# SHANGHAI COOPERATION ORGANIZATION:

## A BOON OR A BANE FOR INDIA AND PAKISTAN

HAROON PASHA

# DEDICATION

I dedicate this humble effort to my affectionate Father Abdul
Rasheed (late) and Mother Naseem Akhtar.

# Table of contents

# Preface

This contemporary world is linked through trade and economic relations. The economic benefits are the main cause of conflict between different countries and they try to accumulate maximum economic incentives through trade and regional integration. Trade agreements are signed to enhance the economic capacities of a country. Regional organizations like NAFTA, E.U and ASEAN are examples of successful models. In this book we will identify the potential threats to confidence-building measures and how can we normalize trade relations with India under SCO's membership.

This book has explored the areas of cooperation between Indo-Pak especially as a member of the SCO organization, which is a trade and regional cooperation organization. Regional organizations like ASEAN and E.U. have done a lot of success in the fields of regional integration and trade. This study shows that how SCO will change the destiny of this region and how the core conflicts can be resolved through the positive application of neo-functionalism. This book explores the new vistas of knowledge and opens new fields of cooperation while utilizing the SCO membership as a catalyst for change. The writer has attended the seminar and National Book Festival to have interaction with the academia and intellectuals for gathering of the data. The work has been enlightening by the talks of different scholars and IR experts. The consultations of different written sources and direct interaction with the scholars have clarified many concepts and enhanced the level of this book.

In April 1996, the five Heads of the States (Russian, Tajikistan, China, Kyrgyzstan and Kazakhstan) joined their hands to sign a historical agreement in Shanghai for strengthening of their military, economic and cultural relations. This was the right step in the path of the 'Alliance of Asia'. After one year all these leaders were agreed to reduce their troops on the border. These confidence-building measures also paved the way for a new level of cooperation and the Heads of the States started their meeting regularly then the minister-level meeting becomes common for addressing the common issues in 2001 this level of cooperation was reached at that level that all the members of the Shanghai Five agreed for a new agreement of SCO. Later on, many other successive agreements were signed by the member States and they signed the agreement for the establishment of SCO. Which is an umbrella organization, under which, a convention for countering terrorism and extremism elimination protection was signed. This book is a humble quest for the search of peace and stability in the region through utilizing the forum of SCO. The future belongs to Asia and this is the 'Asian Century' but it will only become 'Asian Century' when major disputes will be resolve through dialogues and peaceful cooperation. SCO will become the potential forum where the new ties between the Asian giants can mend the historical conflicting ties.

x

# Chapter One

## Introduction

After the devastation of the world wars and major destructions inflected by the man-made lethal weapons, Europe decided to take a new leap forward in the direction of development of the human race therefore in the year 1951 'European Coal and Steel Community was established, it was a time when bloodthirsty enemies joined their hands for cooperation. This Steel community was the shot in the right direction, later this model was followed by the other trade bodies i.e. NAFTA, SAFTA, ASEAN and ECO. It was the first step in the direction of regional cooperation at the international level in recent past. 'Large-scale deaths in WWI and WWII were eye-opening for the world. Euro integration was the right step in the direction of regional cooperation when Europe has joined their hands for large-scale cooperation.

SCO has provided a chance to two nuclear powers neighbouring and belligerent states of South Asia, to establish normal relations with each other. This opportunity could bring economic prosperity, peace and security and social development in this less developed region. Pakistan and India are hostile States like 19th century Germany and France, which always remained in a quarrel with one another at every crucial time, but now they have transformed themselves into friendly and cooperative countries and they are considered as the backbone of the European Union which is a real example of regional integration.

EU has set a new trend of regional integration, by softening borders and abolishing Visa. The theory of neo-functionalism has been applied to it and while applying this theory we can set aside the core issues; the working relations are established based on actual requirements of the trade relations. These relations are made soften with the hostile States based on mercantilism. The main example of this is China, which has a clear policy of 'One China' for Taiwan but they are still having a trade worth US$150 billion, in 2018 and in 2021 Taiwan total exports to China were $188.91 billion. So, it is clear that functionalism explains the necessity of enhancing trade relations especially between hostile States i.e. India-Pak, North-South Korea, Cuba-USA. The world is now a global village and countries are strengthening their economies and maximizing their interest through cross-border trade. Mainland China and Hong Kong accounted for 42% of Taiwan's exports in 2021.

This regional integration has a lot more gains than losses. ASEAN and E.U besides China have made miracles and uplifted the standard of their population and according to the World Bank report more than 850million are pulled out from poverty and made them part of the middle-class community by China. The recent wave of economic warfare between China and the US is based on the concept of national interests which is rising in the west. Trump and post Trump administration is trying to undermine the trade shrewdness of China and raising different types of barriers to stop or slow down Chinese Business. In 2019 world trade was total US$ 42065 billion and E.U had the share of US$5425 billion. In individual countries, America had US$4921 billion and China had US$4342 billion making them the 1st and 2nd biggest traders in the world. SCO member Russia is 19th on the list with US$ 595 billion. The International trade has been increased many folds due to the establishment of the World Trade Organization (WTO), there have been 4018 % growth in world trade between 1950 to 2017 it is almost 40 times.

Since 1995 the world trade value has been expanded up to 4.4% annually till 2017. Due to the best efforts made by the GATT (Later as WTO), there is a 20 % lower in tariffs since 1996 till now. Trade liberalization is the main effort which has been made by different countries to get a hold on their Imports and expand their Exports.SCO has a long history of working for peace and prosperity. The organization is strictly following the rule of non-interference into the internal issues of member States. In the special case of Indo-Pak, it is too early to conclude about the outcomes of the membership's pros and cons. China has been badly trashed by the USA in a trade war and according to BBC US$ 253 billion tariffs is already imposed on Chinese goods and has threatened to impose US$267 billion additional duties on Chinese goods in vice versa China has imposed US$130 billion tariffs on American goods.

Article No 2 of the Shanghai Cooperation Organization (SCO) charter clearly describes that all the member States will respect the sovereignty of members, their independence, respect of borders, non-aggression against members, territorial integrity and principle of non-aggression in all relations. States are given due importance in this organization and all the internal issues of Member States are not discussed. Therefore, according to the charter of SCO, they will not intervene in any internal issue of a State, their principle of non-aggression will be followed in this condition it will be a different forum for India and Pakistan either they are to freeze the heat of Kashmir issue or they are to work for the regional cooperation. According to some experts, there are chances that the SCO would also be dragged into the confrontational politics of India and Pakistan.

The SCO would be divided into the Russian led Indian support group and China supported Pakistan group. The latest event of the alleged 'Balakot Attack' has increased the chances of new series of hostilities between both States and it has increased the influence of the non-state actors and their power to trigger the situation between two belligerent atomic powers. The 'Balakot incident' right after the 'Pulwama attack' has exposed the weakness of the short span bubble of Ufa spirit. Now after many missed opportunities, we have very limited options in hand to resettle the pace of peace because the hostile Modi government in India is very uneasy with the internal changes in Pakistani politics and they believe that India has to unilaterally deal with the non-State actors. The membership of SCO can play a very significant role in dealing with the peaceful resolution of all the disputes and it is the 'Panacea' of all the problems if we tactfully utilize this forum. The world will see an emergence of peaceful and prosperous South Asia, with the help of SCO membership.

The present age is the age of economic integration of different countries into different economic blocs. The organizations like African Union, ASEAN, NAFTA, European Union and SCO have done miracles and they have resolved regional disputes and improved standards of living in these regions. These regional economic organizations are the role model for the countries like Pakistan and India. Pakistan and India had fought three full-scale wars and many skirmishes from their very first day of Independence. The wars and eternal hostilities changed the direction of the governments from the core issues of poverty, illiteracy, terrorism, regionalism, unemployment etc. The new wave of nationalism in India and Pakistanis another problematic phenomenon for resolving the regional disputes. Shanghai cooperation was the organization that was created when the five Central Asian Republics joined this agreement with China and Russia. SCO is the ray and role model for the countries like us to put aside the hostilities and start a new future.

Pakistan has joined SCO with India on 9th June 2017 which itself is an unprecedented act.SCO has opened a new arena of cooperation in the region and it is the biggest threat for already dilapidated control of America in the region, besides that it will create a power vacuum in the region and both Pakistan and India are to cooperate in this regional context, they are to cater for the posing challenges and long journey for their resolution. According to Ex-Foreign Secretary Abdul Basit, there is only 5 % trade between SAARC countries. Despite being geographically close, the rich diversity in member's history, backgrounds, language, national interests, style of government, wealth and culture have at times made the SCO's development and decision making phlegmatic and full of procrastination. The role of the Shanghai Cooperation Organization in future will be based on the opinion of its member States, either they want to see it as a political and military organization, or economic and trade organization. The organization has indeed developed during the past decade however restrictive forces and tough challenges remain. Making the transition from a security alliance to an economic alliance requires a stronger level of trust, commitment, agreement, understanding and legal documentation and one wonders if the SCO is capable of meeting these challenges effectively?

The ongoing conflict in Afghanistan, growth of extremism, need for an improved communication system, need to enhance Russia and China's relationship, demand for trust, increased drug trafficking and illegal immigration are some of the serious internal issues the organization now faces whilst externally dealing with enlargement, managing increasing Foreign Direct Investment (FDI) and better engaging with non-members are clear challenges. Despite the supposed good intention, the SCO's complex environment creates apprehension among members and an environment where 'it is easy for the SCO members to have meetings and arrive at agreements, yet difficult to implement what is written on paper.

Comparative advantage theory is used to check the trade performance of trade organizations. The unhindered economic integration of regional countries under different trade blocs have been a recent development in international trade. It was the year 2001 when SCO was announced in China and the Central Asian countries Kyrgyzstan, Kazakhstan and Tajikistan were the first signatories of this organization with Russia and China. The organization agreement formally came into force in 2003. Uzbekistan abstained itself from membership, right now there are eight full members including India and Pakistan. In 1997 the Chinese premier and Russian President signed a treaty and declared that this world is no more Unipolar and now it is a multi-polar world. The members of this organization are representing half of humanity. The threat of separatism, regionalism and extremism are the core areas of concern.

According to the scholar Richard Rousseau, Indian interests are very different and diverse according to his research he concludes that India has a diverse base of interests in SCO membership and there is a natural link between Indian interests and the scope of the SCO. The three evils are marked as the main threat for the SCO and they are declared as the main threats for the region and three evils separatism religious extremism and terrorism are the topmost priority of the Indian government and it is fighting these evils for a long time. India wanted to jointly fight terrorism while joining the joint exercises with the regional countries. SCO will be very helpful to exchange classified information regarding terrorism. Under this organization, all the important ministries i.e. interior, defence, information and intelligence agencies exchange their information and have regular interaction with one another.SCO has also proposed free trade area for the member States by 2020. All the member states will be economically integrated, which is a strong attraction for India. It is that tempting that India is giving more weightage to SCO than US-supported Asia Pacific Economic Cooperation (APEC). The real issue lies in the factor, that when there will be complete peace in Afghanistan. The observer status is also given to Afghanistan in the 2012 Astana Summit. Pakistan is also unresolved to fully utilize this opportunity by setting aside the USA pressure.

# Chapter Two


## SCO: Pakistan and India


SCO is the resurrection of the Shanghai five and the two heavyweights of the world like China and Russia are the founding members of this organization. Now after becoming India and Pakistan as member of SCO, its importance has increased many folds. Pakistan and India are nuclear powers and economic power of South Asia. They are also the emerging powers of Asia. The importance of SCO has increased many folds after the announcement of the Belt and Road initiative (BRI) by President Xi Jinping of the People Republic of China. BRI has amplified the importance of trade in the world and the strategic vision of the world has been shifting from the mere strategic objectives to the importance of economic/trade relations. BRI will initially connect the 65 countries of the world and around 4 billion people of the world until now, more than a hundred countries and organizations are made part of it (Malik, 2019).

The SCO would be changed into a forum where after securing membership of Pakistan and India would be able to resolve their regional disputes amicably. The core issue of Kashmir can also be resolve through the mediation of China and Russia. This is beyond the charter of SCO to interfere with the regional and internal issues of the member countries. The objectives of the SCO are very clear and they have drawn a line of non-interference of it and the areas of cooperation are also highlighted for cooperation in the fields of separatism terrorism and extremism.

**What is the regional organization?**

After the fall of the USSR, the role of regional organizations has increased many folds. The success of few regional organizations is even phenomenal. The charter of UN Chapter VIII deals with the making and functioning of the regional organizations. Its Articles 52-54 further elaborates on the role and functioning of these regional organizations (United Nations, n.d.).The regional organizations are responsible to manage the territorial conflicts and they use the regional resources at optimum level. Due to their area familiarity, they better manage the local conflicts and support UN Security Council. Regional organizations are the main cause of pacific settling of regional disputes through dialogue or re-engagement at a regional

level. Figure1. SCO member Countries

Source www.insightonindia.com

EU is an example of successfully managing many issues through its forum and active diplomacy. They prevented many storms from gathering and nip the evil in the bud. League of Nations was the first international organization. It was a failed organization, but it was the predecessor of the United Nation which was established in 1945 during WW II. The UN may not be fully successful, but its peacekeeping operations are a role model for NATO and SCO. E.U had taken a step further and made economic integration her motive. Then North American Free Trade Agreement (NAFTA) formed Asia Pacific Economic Cooperation (APEC). UN peacekeeping troops played a decisive role in Bosnia, Somalia Rwanda etc. but she played no role in Kashmir solution, Palestine and during the USA invasion of Iraq. International organizations have different scopes, most international organizations are nongovernmental. Red Cross is a nongovernmental organization and European Union is an example of a regional organization.

**UN Charter and Regional organizations**

Article 51of the UN charter tells that nothing can impair any member State from deciding to safeguard her from war and external threat. The measures which are taken by any member State for self-defence shall immediately come into the notice of the Security Council and the matter shall be immediately discussed by the UN Security Council (UNSC) on principle. The role of the UN has partially sidelined by the USA after adopting the unilateral policies after the 9/11 event (UN legal, 2019).

The UN Charter, chapter VIII Articles 52-54 deals with the arrangements of regional organizations. These Articles clarify the role and functioning of regional organizations under the UN charter. The Articles are;

# Article 52

1. This article provides the legal authority for the establishment of regional organizations and agencies. It clarifies that regional organization and agencies are established where their role in supporting the peace and security of the region. This role should be under the parameters of set principles and purposes of the United Nations.

2. All the efforts should be focusing on the pacific settlement of the regional disputes. The efforts should be started and efforts should be made before the matter is presented to Security Council.

3. The matter for the pacific settlements of the regional disputes should only be brought to the notice of the Security Council after regional arrangements and the matter should directly refer to the State concerned or the Security Council.

4. The application of Articles 34 and 35 are not impaired by this article.

## Article 53

1. The regional organizations should be used for enforcement actions where there is considered appropriate by Security Council. Without the authorization of the Security Council, no enforcement efforts are applied, as it is defined in paragraph 2 of this Article, against enemy State, allowed for consistent to Article 107.

2. When the term enemy State is used, it defines any State which was the enemy during World War II to the signatory of this charter.

## Article 54

International peace can be maintained and security purpose can be achieved when all the regional security arrangements would be in the knowledge of the Security Council (UN, 2019).

Figure2. Different Regional Organizations

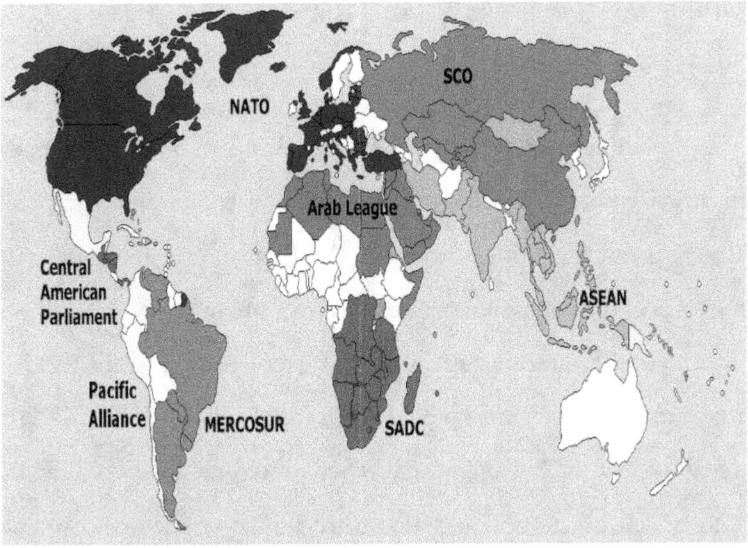

SCO
NATO
Arab League
Central American Parliament
ASEAN
Pacific Alliance
MERCOSUR
SADC

Source www.wikipedia.com

## Chinese Objectives with Pakistan

India and Pakistan is already a member of the South Asian Association for Regional Cooperation (SAARC) since its inception (SAARC, n.d.). The failure of the SAARC to resolve the regional issue at the regional level is not achieved by this organization and its performance is far below the satisfactory level. The failure of this regional setup also shows the volume of mistrust between Pakistan and India. Some scholars are also of this opinion that the fight between these two countries can also off shadow the performance of SCO. According to Dr Reeves, "Such animosity could also develop between India and China or force a division with Russia-India on one side and China-Pakistan on the other" (Reeves PhD, 2014).

Chinese completed the 1st milestone of their journey in 1999 when 50 years of their journey were over with full sovereignty and independence. At that China realized that they are globally emerging as a great power, as an international actor supporting peace and stability with wisdom. They set the role of the global balancer. In the last decade of this 20th century, they emerged as a politically stable, self-confident and economically prosperous country. Their role is ever increasing regionally and internationally (Zaki, 2010). President Xi's ambitious BRI has an eye-opener for the West especially for the US that China is not a less ambitious regional country but it is pulling its socks for a more assertive role in world politics through trade, investment and development. The main offshoot of BRI is CPEC which is passing from Pakistan and bearing the investment of around US$ 68 Billion (Malik, 2019). So after this huge investment, the Chinese stakes are very high in Pakistan. China has not only invested inside Pakistan but aggressively supported Pakistan at all International forums especially in UNSC and while securing membership for

SCO.US is propagating that China is trapping the world in a 'Debt Trap' which is a baseless claim.

Pakistan is a strong supporter and time-tested friend of China. So, China is fully confident about its CPEC investment and after securing the membership of SCO now Pakistan can bridge the land gap between Russia Central Asia and India. Although China has hugely invested inside Pakistan, besides that it has a huge trade of around US$ 80 Billion with India. According to the world trade organization (WTO), there has been 4018 % of world trade, "between 1950 to 2017" almost 40 times. Since 1995 world trade has been expanded 4.4 % annually till 2017. There is a 20 % lower tariff since 1996 due to WTO (WTO, 2019). These trade opportunities have increased regional cooperation and integration. Many western political philosophers believe that the State institutions of Pakistan are very weak and they can't bear a fast economy and structural reforms. According to Professor Francis Fukuyama, "But China is not Nigeria or Pakistan. The central government was able to impose strict discipline on the Township and Village Enterprises (TVEs) in a way that focused their attention on promoting long term growth, like the industrial policies set by other States in East Asia(Fukuyama, 2015).

The SCO is a new experience in multilateral regional cooperation in which security cooperation has preceded economic cooperation. The SCO is gradually making a transition from security-centric to economy centric issues, political stability to energy stability. In addition to six full members, four observers have been added, namely Mongolia, Iran, Pakistan and India. The western countries see the emergence of SCO as a counterweight of NATO's eastward expansion (Zaki, 2010). So, the direction of the Chinese strategy is economics not military based. China is until now an unbeatable player in international trade.

## Pakistan China trade

The Chinese are very shrewd traders and they have intelligently moulded all the trade indicators in their favour. Pakistan is their time-tested friend and their friendship is down reaching the Indian Ocean and superior to the Himalayas. The wisdom of the Chinese is very strong and they easily mould the trade in their favour. The example of Pakistan is also an eye-opener that how the trade is going in the favour of the Chinese.

In 2006, Pakistan and China had signed Free Trade Agreement (FTA) (commerce, n.d.).After FTA, if we have a comparison of trade between two countries. China has surplus trade with the USA because the Chinese are a very intelligent businessman and they are churning from all the trade partners without provoking them. Recently the USA has imposed certain tariff barriers on China which in the same way reciprocated by China. After being a member of the WTO, it is the responsibility of the USA to abide by the rules of the WTO. The free trade agreements are also useful for big industrial countries but it can be havoc for the smaller countries whose industries are under protections.

Table 1.China &Pakistan trade performance after FTA Agreement (2006-2012)

| Dollars (Millions) | Year 2006 | Year 2007 | Year 2008 | Year 2009 | Year 2010 | Year 2011 | Year 2012 |
|---|---|---|---|---|---|---|---|
| Pakistan (Imports from China) | 2915 | 4164 | 4738 | 3780 | 5248 | 6471 | 6688 |
| Imports (Percentage) | 10% | 13% | 11% | 12% | 14% | 15% | 16% |
| Pakistan (Exports to China) | 507 | 614 | 727 | 998 | 1436 | 1679 | 2620 |
| % total share in World Exports | 3% | 3% | 4% | 6% | 7% | 7% | 11% |

Source: Article 'Pakistan and china social and economic relations' by Jafa Riaz Kataria

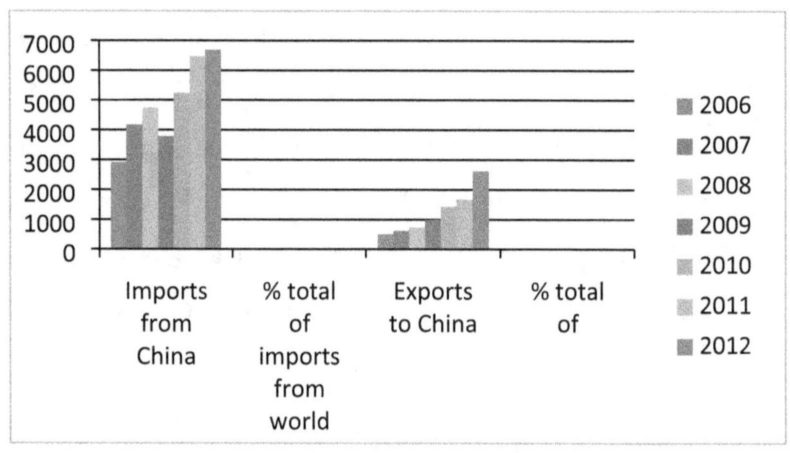


Source: Author

## CPEC and Pakistan

China Pakistan Economic Corridor (CPEC) is not only the game changer but it is the fate changer of this war-torn country. CPEC is going to become the most vulnerable asset of Pakistan in near future. The volume of this investment is huge and the hidden opportunities are limitless for a middle-order economy like Pakistan. Putting all the criticism, scepticism and casting doubt aside, this is the biggest opportunity in the 70 years history of Pakistan which is going to connect energy striven and slowly eroding economy with more than 65 countries or 4 billion people market. India is the most irritating single aspect in the foreign relations of Pakistan and the game between India and

Pakistan is a zero-sum game although the succeeding Pakistani regimes tried their best to change the wrong perceptions of India against Pakistan they but failed. China and it is ever-increasing economic might have changed the dynamics of world politics. Pak-China economic corridor constitutes one of the largest Chinese investments of billions of dollars under the banner of 'Belt and Road Initiative (BRI) (Khan, Malik, Ijaz, & Farwa, 2016). Pakistan has increased its international posture after securing this huge investment. The CPEC will surpass the region of Gilgit-Baltistan and Jumu & Kashmir which is the disputed area claimed by India and it is a constant souring point between India and Pakistan since 1947.

When India will be a part of this project, many of its objections will die down and it will be the partner with Pakistan and China. Western countries are striving hard to place India in front of China as a threat to its trade route. It is very easy for them to create that scepticism that already exists between these two rival Asian nations. The economy of Pakistanis is dependent on the billion dollars CPEC project. This project will connect Gwadar port with the Chinese province of Sinkiang through three thousand road routes passing from three land routes passing from hilly mountains of Pakistan and deserts. Chinese trade with Pakistan, Iran,

Europe, Commonwealth of Independent States (CIS), and Afghanistan will cross the mark of Billions of dollars in the next decade. If only one-fifth of Chinese container traffic will pass through Pakistan, it is estimated that it will generate an economy of billion dollars annually. Indian fears have no grounds even Pakistan can earn from China by attracting them and this trade can be used as a pressure lever for India to soften its Kashmir policy.

Figure4.Map of CPEC Highway Network

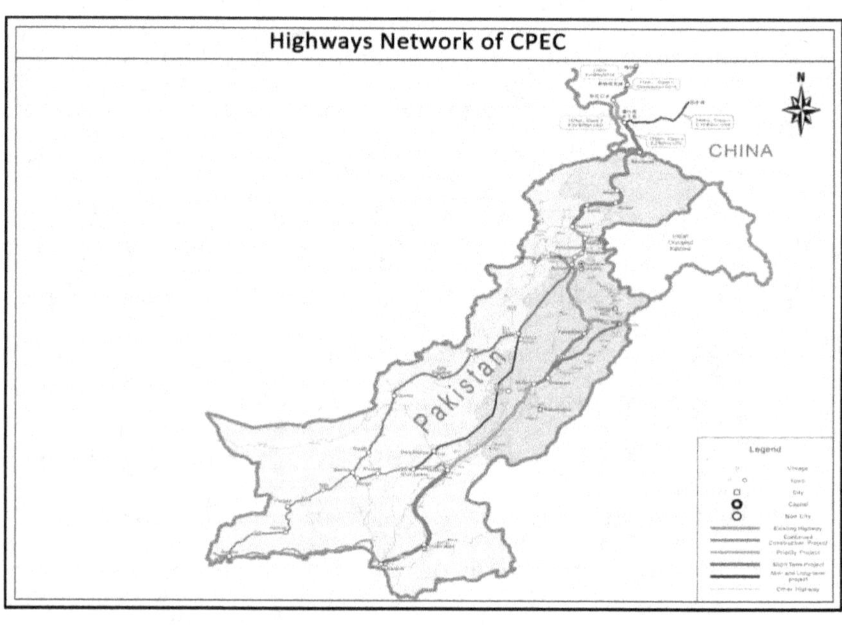


Source www.cpec.gov.pk/maps

Pakistan offers the shortest land route to central Asia if its ports are used which are present on the Arabian Sea.

Moreover, CPEC further extended to the Central Asian States i.e. Kyrgyzstan Tajikistan, Uzbekistan Kazakhstan. Iran offers yet another attractive option to bypass Afghanistan till complete peace. So, the future of Pakistan is in the timely completion of the CPEC and the stability in the region. India can be disciplined by giving a lucrative share in CPEC and land access to Afghanistan but keeping Kashmir in mind.

**How India became a part of SCO?**

From the very first day of its independence, India went closer to China. Nehru was the main architect of these relations and he was the exponent of socialism in India. Members of a political elite class of these two countries had a love for socialism and hate for imperialism, which was their common enemy. Chinese Political class including Chairman Mao had a very positive image of Nehru and the Indian National Congress. The friendship was based on five principles of cooperation, Punj Sheel (five principles of peace)

I.     Territorial integrity
II.    Sovereignty
III.   Peaceful coexistence
IV.    Mutual non-aggression
V.     Mutual non-interference (Arpi, 2015).

But soon the dream of this artificial fraternity was shattered by the Indian imperial transgression in the border region and the Indian Ocean. India fought a regional war with China in1962. All the euphoria of "Hindi Chini Bhai Bhai" was soon evaporated. China and India have one-third of the world population (Lindsay, 2014). Besides these two, Russia and other South Asian countries have almost half of the global population. Pakistan and India both were given the full membership of SCO at the same time and this membership was announced during the Ufa summit. China and India both are members of the BRICS but India has a non-serious attitude about utilizing SCO for resolving the regional disputes (Small, 2015).

## China/ India Economic Profile

India and China are the two primary economies of Asia and emerging economies of the world. The world was made astonished in 2003 when the Indian stock market had been dormant for the previous seven years, suddenly caught fire and yielded returns to investors of up to 350 per cent in a single year. It was an eye-opener for the world. Since then the Indian growth has averaged 9 per cent a year. But the magnanimous growth of India was far behind India (Jha, 2010).

Table 2. China Economic Profile (Economy)

|  | **2000** | **2005** | **2006** |
|---|---|---|---|
| GDP(current US $) | 1.2 Trillion | 2.2 Trillion | 2.7 Trillion |
| GDP (Annual growth %) | 8.4 | 10.2 | 10.7 |
| Exports of goods and services (% of GDP) | 23.3 | 37.3 | 36.8 |

Source: world development indicators database, April 2007

Both the economies are setting new records of growth in the world. China and India are although two different growth models but they have many things in common to analyze their phenomenal growth.

Figure 5. China Economic Profile (Economy)

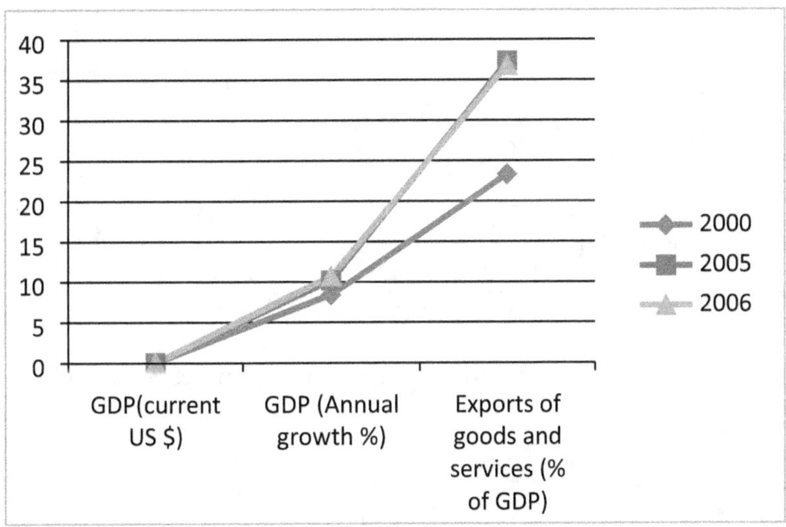


Source: Author.

Here we have a comparison of Indian and Chinese economies. This data is also shown in the abveshown graphical form for a better understanding of the economic profile of the Chinese economy.

This comparison is also showing that India is catching the pace of the Chinese economy and setting new records in South Asia. These two success stories as members of SCO will a boosting factor for many countries especially for the other members of the SCO organization

Table   3.Indian Economic Profile (Economy)

|  | 2000 | 2005 | 2006 |
|---|---|---|---|
| GDP(current US $) | 460.2 Billion | 805.7 Billion | 906.3 Billion |
| GDP (Annual growth %) | 4 | 9.2 | 9.2 |
| Exports of goods and services (% of GDP) | 13.2 | 20.3 | -- |

Source: world development indicators database, April 2007.

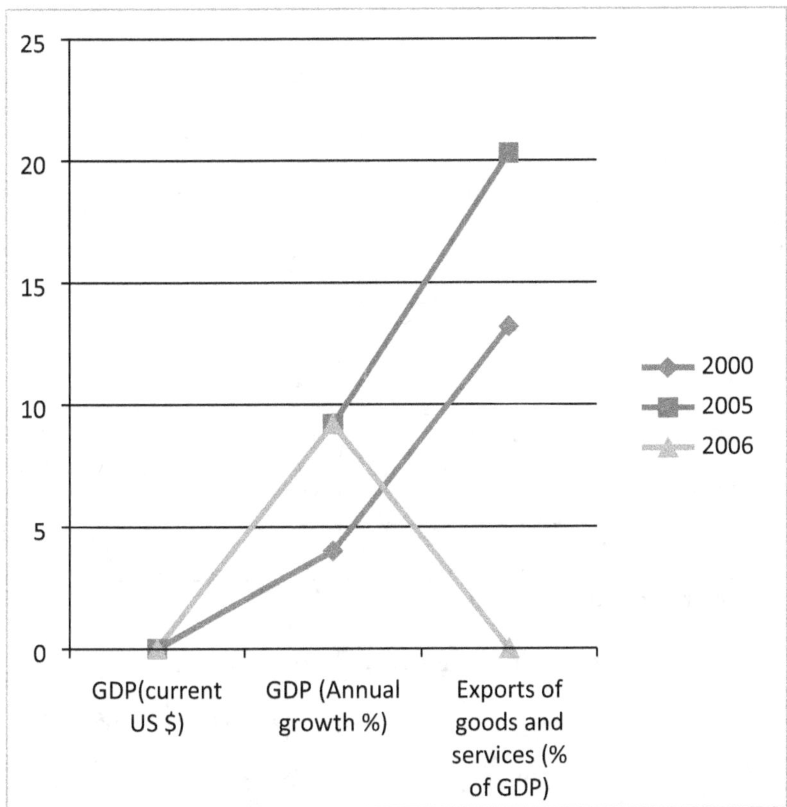


Source: Author.

This data shows that both the member States of SCO are very important player in the economic arena of the world. Their global economic status can also be determined by the consumption of different metals and energy by these global competitors including the USA.

Table   4.Share of China, India and the US in World Consumption (percentage)      key raw materials METALS (2005)

|  | China | India | US |
|---|---|---|---|
| Aluminum | 22.5 | 3.0 | 19.4 |
| Copper | 1.6 | 2.3 | 13.8 |
| Lead | 25.7 | 1.3 | 19.4 |
| Nickel | 15.2 | 0.9 | 9.5 |
| Tin | 33.3 | 2.2 | 12.1 |
| Zinc | 28.6 | 3.1 | 9.0 |
| Iron ore | 29.0 | 4.8 | 4.7 |
| Steel production | 31.5 | 3.5 | 8.5 |

Source:  cited in (Jha, 2010)

Although the massive growth of India and Chinese has created many environmental issues besides other domestic issues like massive urbanization and prices hikes in the urban centre which has increased the inflation in these countries due to unprecedented growth that inflation is being absorbed in the growth rate but the pollution and other issues will create a humanitarian crisis in near future.  Here we have another table of global consumption of US, India and China.

Figure   7. Share of China, India and the US in World Consumption (%) of key raw materials (METALS, 2005)

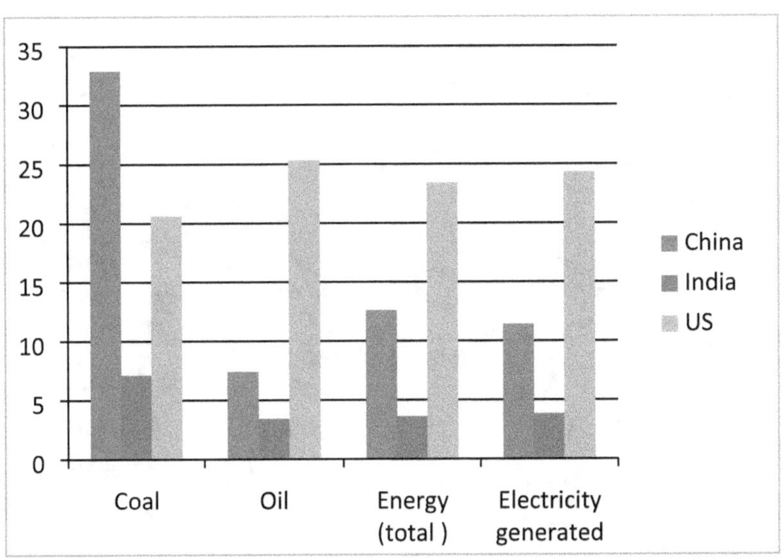


Source: Author.

Table   5.Share of China, India and the US in World Consumption (%) (ENERGY, 2003)

|  | China | India | US |
|---|---|---|---|
| Coal | 32.9 | 7.1 | 20.6 |
| Oil | 7.4 | 3.4 | 25.3 |
| Energy (total) | 12.6 | 3.6 | 23.4 |
| Electricity generated | 11.4 | 3.8 | 24.3 |

Source:  cited in (Jha, 2010)

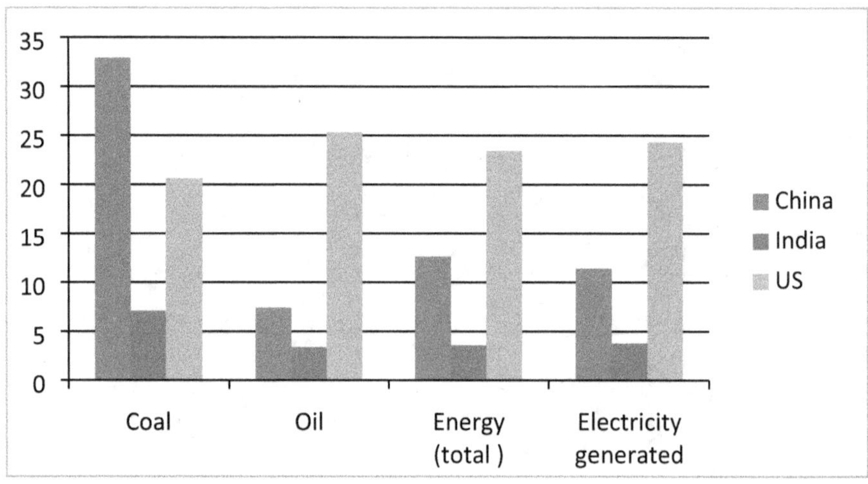


Source: Author.

## Russian Objectives with Pakistan

Although in past the second superpower of the world was Russia and it had a strong influence in the region but after the fall of the USSR, the influence of Russia is dwindling in the region. According to Reeves "While Russia maintains the advantage of having shared linguistic, historical, and cultural ties with the many Central Asian States, these traditional linkages are eroding as younger generations look to Beijing, not Moscow, for the opportunity"(Reeves PhD, 2014).

China is their main trade partner and China has started exploitation of Gas and Oil from this region. Russia under the leadership of Putin has increased their sphere of influence not in the region but globally. Russia wanted to knock out the US from the region at any cost because the US was massively increasing its influence in the region. The US supported the billion dollars TAPI project to diversify the export of the hydrocarbon deposits from the outside region. Besides investing US$ 1.7 billion in the energy sector in Afghanistan US invested US$ 2 billion to build 1800 km national highways (Mcbride, 2015) Other interests of Russia is to broaden its trade with the regional bloc to counterbalance the US economic hegemony in the world. Partially Russia is successful in the Middle East and Latin America where US influence is eroding and China is increasing its presence in Africa while investing in Oil Gas and infrastructure development projects.

SCO can play as a common forum to counter US influence in the region and have a check on the expansion of NATO beyond its actual scope of Europe. Pakistan remained a non-NATO member and supported ISAF led operation in Afghanistan, now Russia is increasing its involvement in the region and first of all, they are trying to decrease Pakistan dependency on the USA. Russia has extended its cooperation in many fields and now the membership of SCO will play a crucial role in the shaping of the future ties between the two countries. All the Russian moves are partially counter by the USA by inviting PM Imran Khan to Washington although the USA move is Afghan solution-centric the long-term objectives are not neglected.

# Chapter Three

## Achievements of SCO

The transformation of SCO from Shanghai five in 2001 was a very noticeable event of the contemporary world.SCO has been conceived as a regional success story and steps in the right direction and it is the window of opportunity. Sustainable development and combating terrorism is the main objective of this organization. The membership of SCO for Pakistan will increase the geopolitical importance of it and will increase its role in the region for the enduring prosperity of the region. There are many dividends and takeaways for Pakistan as an economic regional player. After becoming a member of the trade and energy corridor corridors of China now it is the responsibility of Pakistan to secure the maximum share from the corridor projects and actively developed its diplomacy to resolve regional disputes. Nevertheless, the grant of admission as a member is full of many challenges, linking with a complex geopolitical environment. This research will analyze that after SCO's membership Pakistan and India will utilize this forum for problem-solving and make it more complex.

SCO has successfully promoted regional peace and stability among its member States. SCO has developed a mechanism to promote territorial security and stability of the region and member States. The security apparatus of SCO operates around supporting counter regionalism and extremism. The issues like drug trafficking, smuggling of arms, structured crimes and terrorism are common ills from the region which are sets target of this organization. The alliance regularly takes exercises to enhance efficiency. These military exercises are the indication of cooperation against extremism, separatism and terrorism. Since 2002 many joint military drills have been exercised (Albert, 2019).

Regional Anti-Terrorism Structure (RATS) was initiated in 2002 at Bishkek, later it was shifted to Tashkent in 2004. The RATS is an intelligence-sharing forum against all three evils. The database established against terrorist outfits. Seminars are also organized on curbing terrorism, rendering specialized training with other international security organizations. Besides RATS there are collaborations in many other fields i.e. institution of the judiciary, law enforcement agencies, governmental ministers, Defense ministers, interior minister, Chief of General Staff. Chinese investment in Central Asia is a window of opportunity for these countries. Minerals and energy sectors are the areas of cooperation among China and Central Asia. There is scepticism in Russian about Chinese projects and investment in the region. Russia will not accommodate the Chinese domineering role in the region and world. China is also accommodating the Russian reservations. 'The New Great Game' is going to be played by the international players in the region (Rehman, 2014).

This area of China and the sub-continent was known for the trade and Silk Road was the main road which was connecting thousands of miles of dirt and metallic roads from Canton to the Mediterranean for the trade of Herbs, spices, colourful glass, blue pottery, rugs and of course silk(Albert, 2019). But in the 21st century, the trade items have been changed. Like EU countries SCO is the best available organization which can like the Eurasian zone within itself and with Europe through Russia. The SCO is often considered as the "Association of Asia", due to its special focus on the Asian continent and it has been the main pillar of stability of the region. SCO is considered the most powerful emerging organization in the world because of its power base, which is rotating around the powerful giants of Asia. As the biggest organization, it is covering a major chunk of Asia. The most powerful members of SCO are the leaders of the world like China is the leader in trade and Russia is a leading regional power due to its military might and its ever-expanding role under the leadership of President Putin.

In 2005, SCO had acquired observer status in UN General Assembly and on the UN's 60th anniversary a few months later; the Secretary-General of SCO was invited to make his first speech to UN (DPPA, 2019). It was the acknowledgement that how SCO is increasing its influence and how the world is treating it as a powerful body. Different agreements were signed with the regional and International organization i.e. ASEAN, the Commonwealth of Independent States (CIS) was signed. The other organizations like Collective Security Treaty Organization (CSTO) and the Eurasian Economic Community were signed (Akine, 2010).SCO member states are the central connectivity point of different Central Asian countries and South Asian countries with Afghanistan. Although there is unrest in Afghanistan, due to which it is called Afghanistan Quagmire and up till now there is no evident peace in the region and this will also hinder the success of SCO and ECO in the region even Afghanistan perpetual unrest will hinder the stability in the region and it will further deteriorate the region because without peace in Afghanistan there are very bleak chances of success of SCO especially for Indo-Pak. The USA has not given any clear pull-out policy for Afghanistan

(Williams, 2012). It was and Donald Trump administration of the USA is lacking vision and consistency regarding its policies.

SCO is a beacon of hope for the suppressed regions of Asia. It has contributed not only to the stability of the region but the prosperity of the region is also ensured by the SCO through its agenda. The three major evils are declared the major ills for the member States. The policy of non-interference in the internal affair is another golden principle set by this organization. Territorial stability and economic prosperity are being preserved via collective efforts against the collective evils. Some important aspects of this organization are:

- The Mutual trust is prevailing at the highest level in SCO and special focus has been given to the anti-terrorism setups.
- The three evils, extremism, separatism and terrorism are declared as the biggest challenges for the SCO and drug trafficking and the illegal smuggling of the weapons is marked as the real challenge for SCO as real security challenges for the region.

- Different strata and level of interactions were formed at councils, public prosecutors, supreme judges, interior minister and ministers of defence level were activated. Different sub setups were being organized by this organization and internal affairs, public security and drug agencies head were scheduled to take regular interactions with each other.

- Regional Counter-Terrorism Structure (RATS) was set up in Tashkent to counterinsurgency, terrorism. RATS regularly share the classified intelligence with the member States to enhance their counter-terrorism potential.

- To enhance cooperation with other regional players and to pick up the potential members for the future, regular interaction is done with other countries and dialogue partners by giving them observer status in the organization (Xiaodong, 2012).

SCO has shown significant improvement in three areas of cooperation Firstly, they have achieved a milestone in the field of regional relations, direct contacts are made and mutual antagonism has been reduced Secondly, it has boosted the regional development especially since China has massively invested in the region in energy and infrastructure fields and Lastly, the area has been well politically integrated into 'communion' with rising superpower status. The regional countries have a say in the region by the presence of SCO (Akine, 2010)

## Conflict Management in Asia through SCO

The Asian continent is the second most war-torn continent after Africa. With the help of UN and regional organizations many disputes if not all issues can be resolved because the countries which have locked their horn in disputes have limited capacity to settle their disputes so regional organizations have to fill the vacuum and give peace and opportunity to settle disputes. E.U. and NATO had played this role in Europe for settling many regional disputes. Now SCO is going to play this role in Asia.

Some Western political scholars ridicule the importance of SCO in the region by considering it as a mere showpiece where its member heads of the States gather only for a photo session. According to their observation up till now no solid development has been made by the SCO as an international organization.

## SCO and Afghanistan Quagmire

Afghanistan is the centre of the problems. After four decades of fighting and civil wars now it a breeding ground of extremism, separatism, drugs trafficking and terrorism. The de-weaponization of Afghanistan is the main issue and the ending ISAF mandate was not ended when President Barak Obama presented his 'End game' (Williams, 2012). SCO has to adopt a multipronged strategy to secure all the borders along with Afghanistan i.e. China, Tajikistan and Uzbekistan borders to contain the seeds of extremism and other evils from expansion.

SCO has to strongly support the Afghanistan government to strengthen its base and establish friendly relations with Pakistan and India to open its trade links with them. Pakistan can offer its services to train their Police and Army for countering insurgency and terrorism. Socio-politico-economic challenges can meet with the help of Pakistan. If Pakistan expands the road links of CPEC towards Afghanistan via Qandahar and Jalalabad then it would be the biggest development project for the people of Afghanistan which will connect them internationally with the world through ATT and Pakistani ports.

Figure 9.  Proposed Rail/Road Linkages with Afghanistan

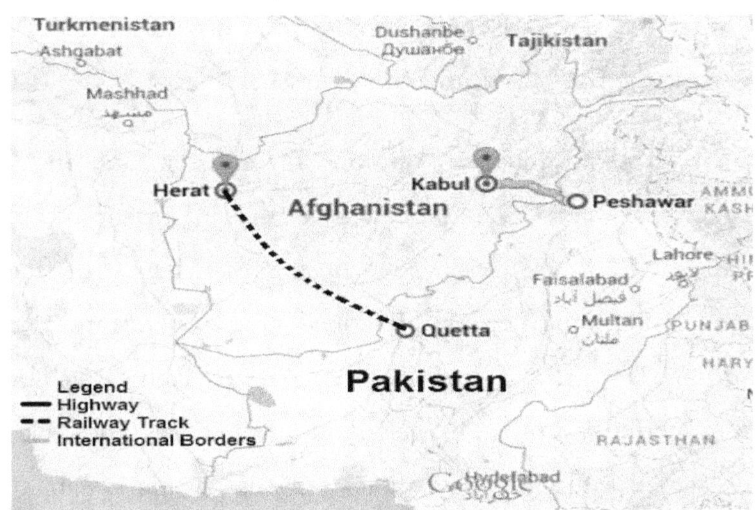


Source : www.criterion-quarterly.com/afghanistan-pakistan-trade-investment-roadmap/

SCO should focus on this issue because the strategic location of Afghanistan is very important and all the major land connectivity projects i.e. CASA and TAPI would be passing from it. Afghan Transit Trade (ATT) can be made as to the part of CPEC and the network of Pakistan motorways can be extended to Kabul. Railways and highways can link it from Qandahar and Jalalabad.

## Indo-Pak disputes and potential role of SCO

There is a long chequered history of fragile relations between two hostile States of Indo-Pak. SCO is a forum that can provide them with a platform where they can start a new journey towards peaceful settlements of the disputes. For the chronic issues of Kashmir, Siachen, water disputes, SCO can become the panacea against all these issues.

SCO is a beacon of hope for Pakistan and India. Therefore, the SCO has become a very important forum addressing all the socio-politico-economic issues of the region. SCO has clearly described that sovereignty; the territorial integrity of every member State is taken care of by non-interfering in the internal affairs of the State. The issues are settled through consultations. SCO is playing a stability factor role for the region and it is standing against the western subjugation of the hydro-carbon resource of the Eurasian region. Gradually SCO has been developed into a powerful region player. SCO has devised a multidimensional roadmap for the development and prosperity of the region. SCO will focus on those principles which will ensure the free flow of goods and services. The routes for the trade would be channelized. The transportation and energy sectors are given due focus and regional members will ensure it. SCO has maintained the credibility of a powerful regional player by its neutral role through its noninterference in the internal issues but can it be a powerful forum to resolve our regional disputes?

SCO strongly discourage its forum to be utilized for quarrels then how can Pakistan and India utilize this forum for peaceful settlements of their disputes? There is a prevailing scepticism in the minds of different scholars and few are of this opinion that SCO may be changed into two opposite camps after the entry of Pakistan and India into it (Reeves PhD, 2014).

**Areas of cooperation under SCO**

Pakistan enjoys a pivotal position in South Asia due to its strategic location which connects Central Asia with South Asia onwards to South East Asia. It has the shortest ground links with Central Asia and its presence in the Arabian Sea from where seventy percent of the world oil is shipped and has increased the role of its many folds. The geopolitical, geo-economic and geo-strategic credentials are quite bright for it because it enjoys the natural link between SCO and the rest of the world. Pakistan enjoys the shortest land access to Central Asia and its links with the warm waters of the Arabian Sea. The trade and commercial connectivity make it the big player in the region. After becoming a member of SCO Pakistan will strengthen the North-South trade and energy corridor passing through Gwadar.

SCO will not only be strengthening the existing links but will also open new horizons in the fields of regional integration and cooperation. The energy striven countries like India and Pakistan will link themselves with the energy hub of Central Asia. SCO and its member States like the Central Asian States can fulfil the maximum needs of India and Pakistan. The TAPI and CASA projects will add up the electricity and hydrocarbon resources of the region. These projects will open a new milestone in the history of Asian cooperation (Cohen, 2006).

The counter-terrorism expertise of SCO will be very helpful for India and Pakistan to share their experiences. The SCO is against any kind of meddling in the domestic issues of the associated member States. Extremism is the other evil of this region which can be counted with the collective assistance of SCO. The rise of SCO is the manifestation of the emergence of a new century which is the Asian Century. SCO is a forum that will be used for the economic integration of its member States for that purpose another organization naming Eurasian Economic Union (EEU) has already been established in 2014. There are many hidden incentives in the membership of SCO and its umbrella organizations. The economic integration projects like China Pakistan Economic

Corridor (CPEC) and Belt and Road initiative (BRI) will be the fate changer for India and Pakistan. (Aris, 2008)

There are a lot of cynical views about the performance of the regional organizations. The unsuccessful international organizations like ECO, OIC and SAARC have many stories to share but the successful organizations like ASEAN, NAFTA and E.U have outshined the stigmatized regional organizations through their performance. International organizations should be treated as important players in regional politics. The sovereignty of the State is not at stake, due to the ever-expanding role of the regional organizations. The regional blocs like ASEAN and European Union have deeply netted their populations into a closely integrated economic union which is mutually beneficial for every member country.

The new form of global governance has emerged due to the presence of international organizations and regional organizations. These international organizations are not necessary for international politics. The areas of cooperation are diversified by these organizations. Free trade agreements, visa-free regimes, artificial integration, knowledge economies, and industrial complexes are developed through different regional agreements. After the ever-increasing role of the World Bank, (WB) and International Monitory Fund, (IMF) and the debate of the legitimacy of the regional and international organizations have gathered momentum. The less integrated regional organizations like ASEAN and South American trade bloc 'Mercosur'(The regional organization of South American countries)are considered as suitable regional organizations and successful model of regional organizations.

## SCO and Pakistan: A Way Forward

From the very first day of its inception, Pakistan was in search of true friends. Pakistan tried to establish its links with the west by joining SEATO and CENTO. Later on, Pakistan blindly cooperated with the USA for making its western allies happy; even they spared their land for espionage against communist countries due to which the U-2 incident happened. These unholy alliances and search for friends had thrown us into the war of Afghanistan. These entire unsuccessful searches for alliances and friendship were futile and useless even these efforts created undue foreign policy hurdles. Bangladesh was forcefully separated from Pakistan due to our illicit link with the west but nobody came forward to help us. After all these episodes of unhappy relations, Pakistan was in search of membership of a pragmatic forum for regional cooperation.

There is no comparison of SCO, except with the organization like NAFTA and EU. These organizations are older and more resourceful than SCO. Now Western countries had shifted their focus to Central Asia due to its hydrocarbon resources and proximity. The presence of Pakistan and India as fully capable nuclear States will increase the importance of this organization many folds. The importance of Pakistan in the Muslim world and her influence in OIC will be a force multiplier for SCO (Greg, 2004).

After the Shanghai cooperation Organization's Dushanbe meeting it was proposed that Pakistan, India, Iran and Mongolia will become the future members of SCO. India and Pakistan have achieved this and have become full members of SCO, on 09 June 2017 in Astana during the SCO session; Pakistan and India were given full status of membership by SCO. PM Pakistan was being welcomed by the SCO Secretary-General. Prime Minister Nawaz Sharif while addressing the summit, said, "The SCO goals resonate with Pakistan's national ethos, and so do the core values of the Shanghai spirit and the SCO charter, with our quest for a peaceful neighbourhood." (APP, 09 June 2017). It was miraculous news for Pakistan after singing the CPEC another door was opened for Pakistan and there were many expectations from entrepreneurs to Industrialists and students to political workers who were very happy. It was a leap forward in the right direction.

The membership of the SCO will be a treasure trove for Pakistan in future.SCO will be used as a central forum not only for economic policymaking but for resolving regional and territorial disputes. Pakistan is an ideally located country on the map. It connects Central Asia, South Asia and the extended Middle East. The importance of Pakistan is very bright as far as the geo-strategic, geo-economic and geo-political dimensions are concerned. Pakistan is a natural link between the Central Asian Republics, Arabian Sea, SCO countries and the Middle East countries. Pakistan can play a central role to link the North-South energy corridor and trade routes through Gwadar port. CPEC is a new link that can not only enhance the soft image of Pakistan but also will enhance the trade controlling power of Pakistan. After joining SCO, the energy crisis of Pakistan will recede through CPEC energy projects. The old stalled projects like TAPI (Turkmenistan-Afghanistan-Pakistan-India) for the energy starving people of this region. When India will be a stakeholder in this project then it will enhance the stature of Pakistan in the region because Pakistan will be controlling the transit route of these energy projects which will increase the economic vulnerability of India alongside its dependency on Pakistan.

Figure 10. TAPI Gas Pipeline

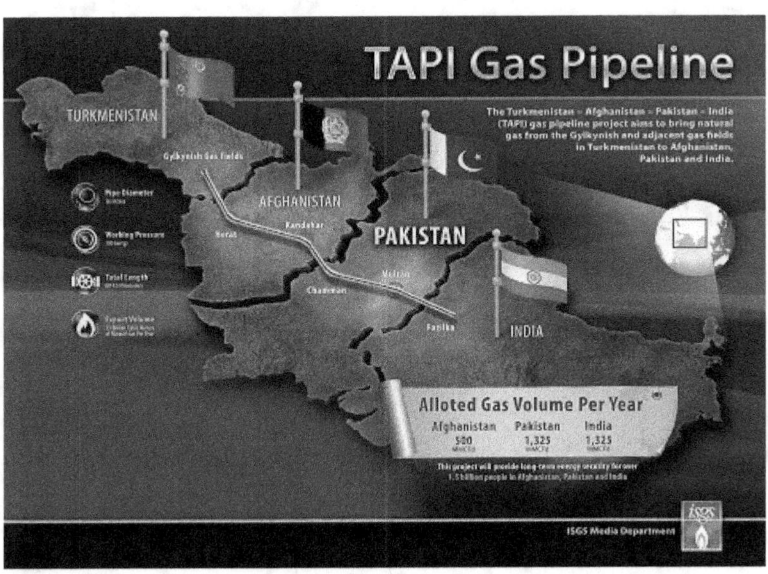



Source www.isgs.com.pk/projects/tapi

SCO will become that forum where we can start a composite dialogue with India. Pakistan can improve relationships with Russia through SCO. Pakistan will play a more assertive role in regional politics and its role in Afghanistan will be a maker, not a breaker. The rehabilitation process in Afghanistan can be initiated through SCO. Health, education and social sector can be improved through SCO. The common enemy like terrorism can be eliminated through joint training and exercises. Pakistan can also strengthen its security apparatus through SCO (Rehman, 2014).

**Linking Central Asian republics with South Asia?**

China has strong interests in the region of Central Asia. This area is situated at the border of China. This region has been considered under the 'sphere of influence' of China. The Russian Federation is also keen to maintain its control in the region, which was a part of the Soviet Union. The United State and other Western countries have also entered the region (Zaki, 2010).

Figure 11.CASA Project Map

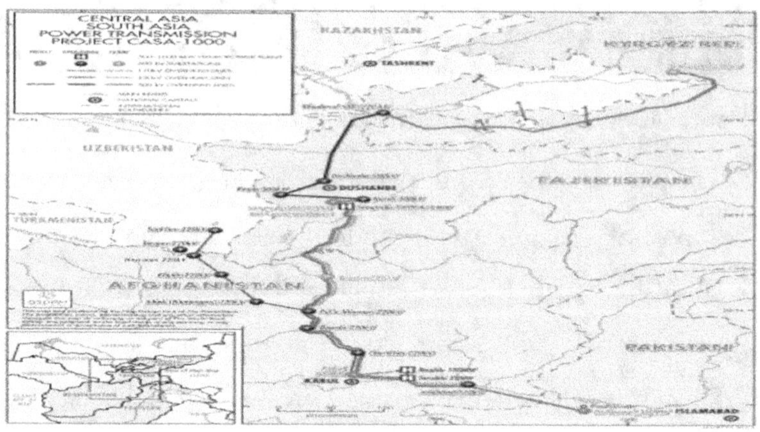

Source        https://www.researchgate.net/figure/Proposed-CASA1000

Many international powers have a powerful presence in the region. Russia is enjoying its historical and cultural dominancy in the region but China is technically replacing it due to its massive economic growth and China has opened an energy corridor with Central Asia. Although historically Central Asia was linked with South Asia due to the Czarist Russian expansions and later on Communists 'Iron Curtain' had delinked this region from the world especially from the Muslim identity and South Asia. After the fall of the USSR in 1991, there were bright chances of melting of the artificial barriers and opening up new relations with South Asia but soon this euphoria was evaporated. There were many reasons why warm and cordial relations were not established between Central Asia and South Asia i.e. old regimes, terrorism, and extremism

Figure   12. Belt and Road Initiative (BRI) linkages

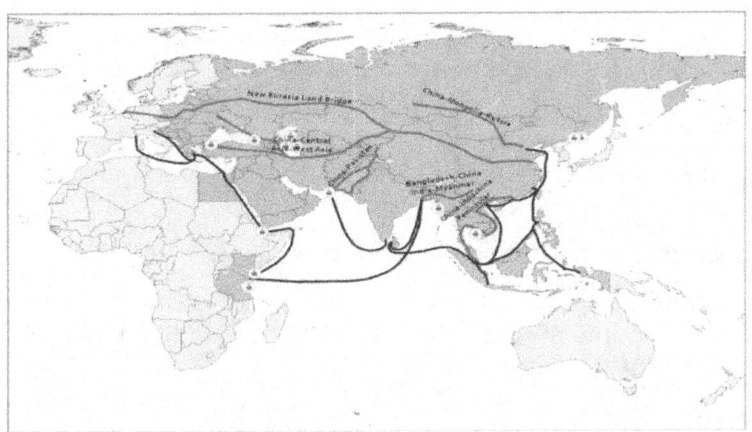

Source www.voxeu.org/article/welfare-effects-belt-and-road-initiative

In the past US was trying to establish links of Central Asia with South Asia and the US facilitated many projects like TAPI and CASA-1000 but China was the major regional power that established practical ground and Air links with Central Asia and further extended those links with South Asia.

BRI is the main project which is going to link four Billion world's population and it will generate the economy of Trillions of dollars in the world. China is following the policy of multilateralism. Beijing is desperately making efforts to curtail the influence of the US in the world, for this purpose China is trying to control the economic lifeline of the world. It is the beauty of Chinese foreign policy that it is following the pragmatic foreign policy and following the neo-functionalism theory in its international trade agreements. China has created a safe zone around itself via signing different trade and security SCO, ASEAN+1 and Asian Regional Forum (Kucuk, 2009).

**Achievements of SCO in Central Asia**

Although the scope of SCO is very limited according to its manifesto the success of SCO is matchless, it can do miracles in future because of this it has changed the perception of the world about this region.SCO has positively engaged all the regional actors and decreased the tensions among the regional countries, on the other hand, China and Russia are dominating the region in a new colonial way.

SCO has been ridiculed by many western scholars because of the lack of will to act, which is prevailing in the mechanism of this organization. This is portraying a very shortsighted approach. Because the SCO members and their territories are very impoverished Although China and Russia are very powerful countries and they are exerting their influence on the region to gain control over the region and counter USA influence. Islamist militancy and poverty are the hallmarks of this region which is called Central Asia or Turkistan (old name of the region). The power of Russia and China are not fully utilized till now that's why the region is facing an acute shortage of the collective mechanism to counter these problems. The major economic and social programs are not started till now after the breakup of the USSR and still China is lingering behind to fill these gaps although China is the only country that can fill the gap because Russia is not economically that strong.

The world has this realization that although this area is a poor region this area is full of natural resources especially oil and Gas can change the destiny of this area through investment and proper utilization of the earning for social welfare. The main idea behind Chinese diplomacy and Russian diplomacy is that, they are to shift their focus not only on trade incentives but also, they can change the destiny of this region through development projects. Only North American Free Trade Agreement (NAFTA) and the EU, have the potential to greatly impact the lives of their people so much like SCO. Besides, Central Asia has become an area of suddenly sensitive strategic concern to the USA and Western powers. Now Pakistan has become a member of the SCO which has greatly increased the importance of this organization. The impact of SCO will be greater because of the military and economic potential of Pakistan and its influence on the Muslim world. The North American Free Trade Agreement (NAFTA) is a trade agreement and its members are United States, Canada, and Mexico; it went into effect on January 1, 1994. It is the biggest free trade market of three countries at that time measured $6 trillion and directly affected more than 365 million people. NAFTA was created to eliminate tariff barriers to services, manufacturing, and agriculture; to remove investment restrictions; and to protect intellectual property rights (Inc Encyclopedia, 2019).

Russia is not focusing on the SCO for expanding its influence in the world and the region because Russia has this strong realization that China is the economic leader of the world. Russia is going to utilize this organization for protecting its nearest region from extremism, militancy and western expansionism. The priority tasks of the development of the Armed Forces of the Russian Federation, a security policy document published in October 2003. The Russian is taking SCO as beneficial for their geopolitical interests and it is favouring 'Primakov doctrine' which is based on the doctrine to make Russia as the central power of the world politics (Laumulin, 2006).

The Shanghai Cooperation Organization for the first time was discussed in detail. In this 'White Paper,' the SCO was considered as an important organization for regional security and stability in the Central Asia Republic (CARs) and the Far East, especially in countering military threats and militancy. SCO can fulfil many Russian policy objectives especially when Russian is under the control of the authoritarian regime of Putin. Iran, China and India have special economic relations with Russia. These three States have strong strategic relations with Russia and they are the buyer of Russian arms. China and India are bilaterally exercising with the Russian forces for a long. Iran has recently joined them and it proves how ambitious Russia is to expand its strategic influence (Haas & Putten, 2007).

# Chapter Four

## Opportunities for Indo-Pak

Pakistan and India have spent a lot of time quarrelling with one another and fighting full-fledged wars to proxy wars. Now we are living in the 21st century and now it is a time to address the real issues of South Asia. After so many devastations, inflicted by the wars, now it is time to give peace and cooperation a chance. There are lots of opportunities available some out of which are as under:-

### Indo-Pak Trade Maximization

Free trade is the main object of the SCO and economic liberalization is also in the benefit of China because China is a leading country in the world in trade and the Chinese Dragon has awakened from sleep. Economic cooperation not limited to simple trade and not only focusing on trade but: fighting poverty will also finish the grounds of the 'three evils', i.e. terrorism, separatism and extremism. Improving economic incentives and opportunities are the responsibility of SCO, which have been focusing on this agenda item from its inception. The trade between India and

Pakistan is already underutilized and it can be increased up to US$ 37 Billion. According to a World Bank report, the informal trade between two countries is 91 % of the total trade (Mishra, 2018). There are many major fields of cooperation among the member States which are trade, telecommunication, intelligence, information technology etc. trade and investment facilities are also enhanced through this interaction (Haas & Putten, 2007).

**External involvement minimization**

The role of the USA has been challenged by Beijing and Moscow through political, social and strategic alliances. China and Russia believe that they must be taken on board while taking decisions about the region. Beijing is playing the intermediary role in the eyes of the west because of their hatred for Russians. Russia is double-minded about the intentions of China and they are confused about the oil pipeline construction between Siberia and Daqing (Chinese). Russia and China have collectively rejected the USA interventions in Central Asia and its long-term presence in Afghanistan. Kyrgyzstan has allowed the United States to retain its base at Manas (in 2014 it was handed over to the Kyrgyz government). NATO is a powerful organization and it is operating in Africa, Asia and Europe in a different guise but SCO is still in infancy and after the tense relations of

India and Pakistan has also decreased the importance of this organization for them because this organization can't intervene in the integral affairs of its member countries. Except for Afghan, the regional players have limited the American intervention in the region and the regional resources are channelized for the welfare of the States through their sale by competitive bidding. So partially this organization has contained the western influence.

## Resolution of Political Dispute

Many political thinkers were of this opinion that Pakistan and India should resolve their problem like Kashmir first to become members of the SCO. Because without resolving the Kashmir issue the membership of SCO will not be beneficial for us. Due to the spillover effect, it is also assumed by the scholars that Pakistan and India can cause polarization in the SCO, which can easily divide this organization into Chinese and Russian camps (Reeves PhD, 2014). Now without resolving the Kashmir issue the membership of this organization for Pakistan and India is a test case for SCO and its founding members. The populations of China and India have been estimated at 37 % of the world population. Currently, China is home to about 1.4 billion and India has 1.3 billion. It totals more than 2.7 billion in number (Hurworth, 2019). The nuclear power of

India and Pakistan, along with the mineral resources of Central Asia will make this organization the rich and powerful organization of the world, which has the potential to counter NATO.

Figure 13. Map of Kashmir

Source www.google.com

The emerging economies of China, Russia and India could counter the balance economies of the United States and its western allies. The use of the Yuan as an international currency among these countries will further counter the power of the Dollar as an international currency and it will weaken the American hegemony and dominancy (Hughes, 2014).

## Reduction in Arms Race

As a regional organization, the reduction in the arms race is not the primary focus of the organization but its primary focus is on trade and anti-terrorism activities. Separatism and fundamentalism are also pointed out as the threat to regional peace. Kyrgyzstan and Uzbekistan provided military facilities for the US-led coalition's operations in Afghanistan in 2001 right after the establishment of SCO. NATO and the USA are utilizing their presence in Central Asia to gather intelligence, counter fundamentalism and logistics support for ISAF forces in Afghanistan. Kazakhstan was the first Central Asian country who established friendly relations with the west and sent its forces to Iraq also. So, the Central Asian states are also pursuing independent foreign policies and their known examples are Turkmenistan, Uzbekistan etc. who have strong control over their domestic policies and have an independent foreign policy.

SCO have identified extremism, terrorism, insurgency and the drugs pedaling besides other threats and to smash these threats countermeasures are taken. Islamic radicalism is another threat to this region. Since 2002 the situation in Afghanistan has aggravated the law and order situation in the region. China and Russia were partially failed to preserve the law and order situation in the region because initially they reluctantly helped these States and necessary equipment was not provided in time. Anti-drug trafficking exercises efforts have brought limited fruits especially the black market of Afghanistan has opened many challenges for the whole region. So now Pakistan and India set this example of Central Asia and like Russia and the USA, they are to start arms limitation dialogue so that they can set budgets for poverty alleviation and according to Times of India the direct defence spending of India in 2018 was US$58 billion and Pakistan was US$ 11 billion which consists 2.1 % of Indian GDP and 3.6 % of Pakistan's GDP of the same year. So, SCO can a platform through which a new era of cooperation will start (Times of India, 2019).

**Increase in Social Welfare**

After the 2005 Astana summit, the SCO openly started showing its anti-unipolar policies to the world. The Astana declaration of 2005 said that a rational and just world order must be based upon consolidation of mutual trust and good-neighbourly relations, upon the establishment of true partnership with no presence to monopoly and domination in international affairs. Russian and Chinese heads also blamed few international powers who are creating their client States by dominating independent States. Social welfare projects are the hallmark of welfare States in the past

Communist States were also known for their social development and social welfare. China has successfully uplifted 850 million people from poverty into the middle class (World Bank, 2019). This is the biggest example of when the population of such magnanimity was uplifted from poverty into the middle class in a single generation.

According to World Bank and IMF, there was 21.9 % poverty in India and 29.9 % in Pakistan. The per capita income in Pakistan was US$ 1510 and in India, it was US$ 1584(Livemint, 2016). The example of China was miraculous when million were pulled out from poverty now the million people of Pakistan and India can be pulled out through social development while investing in human capital.

The western powers are constantly blaming China for its human rights abuses in Hong Kong, Tibet and Sinkiang regions. They blame China and Russia for abusing the basic right of free speech in their countries and using SCO's platform for not interfering in their internal matters of other member States. All the countries of the world have different cultures, values and political/social systems which had been developed over the years in the process of evolution of human consciousness. All the Central Asian countries are facing the menace of terrorism which is foreign supported by the non-state actors because of the oppressive tactics of the autocratic regimes.

The SCO is culturally active in the region also in the 2004 Tashkent Summit declared that SCO members all have their distinctive human resources that represent a good potential for cooperation. Cooperation should be actively promoted in the fields of culture, education, science and technology, tourism, mass media, etc. to enhance the mutual understanding and friendship among the SCO peoples and consolidate the social basis of the growth of the SCO. The shanghai summit focused on cultural cooperation, people to people contact etc.

**Elimination of Extremism, Terrorism and Separatism**

The three main evils of the regions are marked as the target of SCO and different declarations and signed by the member States. These agreements and declarations are as under

- Shanghai Cooperation Organization Charter was signed on June 15, 2002.
- The Concept of Cooperation Between the SCO Member States on Combating three evils of

- Separatism, Terrorism and Extremism were signed on5 June 2005.

Another Treaty on long term good neighbour treaty was signed between the member states of the Shanghai Cooperation Organization on August 16, 2007.

- On June 16, 2009, the Anti-terrorism convention was ratified by the member States. This forum arranged a convention of SCO against the three main evils.

- In 2007-09 the practical procedure was adopted to suppress the three major evils but the joint efforts made by the member States.

- On June 27, 2007, joint military exercises were conducted by the forum to curb terrorism and upgrade the member response.

- On 28 August, 2008the agreement on cooperation among the officials of the member states of the Shanghai Cooperation Organization on combating illegal circulation of weapons, ammunition and explosives was signed by the member States.

- On16 June 2009, the anti-terrorism training protocol was signed by the member States.

- On 15 June 2006, the Information Security Statement was signed by the head of the States (Xiaodong, 2012).

After joining SCO now this forum is the last refuge for the war-torn countries like us to use this forum to end threats of terrorism, extremism and separatism. The right-wing extremist groups existing in Indo-Pak can be eliminated systematically. SCO is a forum that has a clear cut agenda against all these evils.

## Prospects for Indo-Pak

Many hidden opportunities are lying ahead in the field of cooperation between India and Pakistan. Only there is the requirement of taking the right step in the right direction. We have a long history of the missed opportunities but now after securing the membership of SCO on the same date and time, it has opened the doors for new countless opportunities in different fields. This forum has new prospects for hostile State and these prospects are;

## Regional Disputes

The areas of divergence are many between India and Pakistan but areas of cooperation are very limited.

The seventy years history of tumultuous relations had paved the way for a historical antagonism between the two States. India and Pakistan had fought 3 full-scale wars and many skirmishes, besides that Kashmir, Siachin, Sir Creek, terrorism and Water disputes are also the common areas of hatred. India has diversified and revisited its relations with other Asian countries and also signed many treaties and accords with many countries.

India was made a member of the Nuclear Supplier Group (NSG) with the help of the USA and the nuclear deal was inked between the two. Six nations' Mekong-Ganga Cooperation was launched by India and Cambodia, Laos, Myanmar, Thailand, and Vietnam are the member of this organization. The euro model of economic integration was successfully launched by many Afro-Asian and Latin countries. The East Asian Free Trade Area would comprise of 16 member States, representing 50 % of the world population and having a combined GDP of over US$8 Trillion.

Source https://deacademic.com/dic.nsf/dewiki/18847

China would be able by this EAFA organization to churn the maximum economic benefits because the trade between China and ASEAN is ever-increasing and that is making progress by leaps and bound. In 2005, ASEAN was China's largest partner, standing at no fifth and having a trading volume of US$ 130 billion; while China, in 2005, was set to out-trade the U.S. as ASEAN's largest trade partner. On the other hand, ASEAN has made a total investment of $34bn in China. (Niazi, 2006) World relations are now based on trade and business and the old strategic thinking of the world is changing and the ever-increasing Indian economic and trade relations are a challenge for Pakistan but with this changing world this Zero-sum game can be changed into a positive-sum game

## Political Settlement of Kashmir Issue

The mother of all problems between India and Pakistan is Kashmir and it is that souring wound that is changing into cancer for the mutual relations. The unconstitutional occupation of India over Kashmir since 1947 has many episodes of ups and down even altogether wars over this territory. Now in a recent development, India has revoked Article 370 which was although temporary but the special status to Jammu and Kashmir was tarnished which Kashmir was enjoying since 1954. Article 35A defines that the people of Jammu and Kashmir live under a different set of laws, starting from citizenship, property ownership, and other fundamental rights are different from the members of other States and Indian citizens. Indian citizens can't purchase land or property in Kashmir. The scrapping of special status and the Balakot incident has intensified relations between two nuclear States. Pakistan has tried its best and even Pakistan has returned the captured Indian pilot.

Although there are many missed opportunities still, we have ample opportunities to have a good start of a composite dialogue that is internationally supported and

Russia China and the USA guaranteed. Both the countries have to follow the look forward policy now to materialize their economic target meet. The energy resources of Central Asia can easily divert towards South Asia for the underprivileged population of the SAARC region. The Kashmir solution especially a peaceful solution is necessary to make this area land of peace and cooperation. The narrow nationalism should be set aside and internationalism should be promoted and the theory of functionalism should be kept in mind for greater cooperation among the regional countries. The agreement like the 'Lahore declaration' was a good starter and after that, to date, no other solid agreement has been made by belligerent States.

**Trade Tribulations**

Trade disparities also exist between the regional countries and there is limited trade between the two regional rival countries, India and Pakistan. China is the trade wizard in the world; even India is performing far lower than China. There is historically antagonism between India and China also. The (under shown) chart shows the exports and imports of different trade blocs of the world. Since the 1962 war, the relations between these two countries are not normal but China has established warm relations with Pakistan. China has established warm economic relations with all the South

Asian countries including India. A substantial amount of investment was made through CPEC in Pakistan and BRI was the main economic opportunity for investment in Bangladesh, Sri Lanka and Nepal. (Niazi, 2006).

Table   6.Imports Exports of Economic Unions

| Year | Exports 1995 | Exports 2000 | Imports 1995 | Imports 2000 |
|---|---|---|---|---|
| SAARC | 4.41 | 4.46 | 2.36 | 3.90 |
| NAFTA | 20.93 | 26.70 | 10.89 | 7.33 |
| European Union | 29.18 | 27.14 | 24.59 | 21.14 |
| ASEAN | 6.39 | 4.67 | 13.91 | 13.74 |
| N.E. Asia* | 10.43 | 6.30 | 8.82 | 11.87 |
| ROW | 28.67 | 30.56 | 39.43 | 42.02 |

Source: IMF, Direction of Trade Statistics Yearbook, various issues.
Note:  *North East Asia: China, Japan and the Republic of Korea. ROW= Rest of the World

The trade and investment opportunities are present between India and Pakistan according to one estimate the present trade between two countries can jack up to US$ 37 billion when tariffs are eliminated. Pakistan worked on CPEC and it was materialized in 2013 but before, it India already has started an indigenous trade programme in August 2007when two industrial corridors were approved by the Indian cabinet. The first was to be a gigantic 1,843 km long industrial corridor connecting Delhi with Mumbai. This was to be developed with the Japanese collaboration, with a projected investment of US $ 100 billion. The second corridor was to be between Chennai and Bangalore and was designated to attract US$ 50 billion. This first project was to give benefit to six States. India was much proud to announce that in contrast to China, where half of the investment in joint ventures has been raised abroad, in India the foreign component of foreign direct investment (FDI) can be as low as one-sixth(Jha, 2010).

India is receiving the huge bulk of FDI due to its corporate success that Mercedes, BMW, Chanel, Hugo Boss, Swarovski, Mont Blanc, Louis Vuitton and most of the other global brands arrived in India and the purchasing power of the urban class has increased many times (Jha, 2010).

**Prevailing Skepticism**

The region of the previous USSR was not an attractive market for India because of its out of proximity and tough borders. Pakistan is another barrier for India which exists between the Indian and Central Asian landmass. The India trade volume is just US$200 million. Half of the trade was done with Kazakhstan only. Indian investors are massively investing in the new market i.e. Laxmi Mittal has established a 5.5 million tons steel plant in Kazakhstan..

Firgure 15. TAPI Project MAP

Source https://isgs.com.pk/projects/tapi/

He is eyeing the Chinese market. In May 2006, Turkmenistan-Afghanistan-Pakistan India (TAPI) gas pipeline project was amounting to US$ 5 billion was signed by Pakistan, India, Afghanistan and Turkmenistan. Due to the fear of terrorism India has established its first airbase in Tajikistan. This is the first Indian outpost outside its mainland. Now it is time for India should have a check on its ambition of global dominancy and it has to be focused on the issues of regional development with the help of Pakistan.

**Strategic Issues**

There is a miss conception in the Indian strategic circle that the expansion in Chinese influence will decrease

Indian influence in the region, especially in the Indian Ocean region. Recently China has established their first military post in Africa (AP, 2019). China wants to protect its trillion-dollar BRI project but the west and India have scepticism about it. Through the SCO forum, the prevailing negativity and scepticism among neighbouring countries can be addressed. SCO is a forum that has established the border of peace among its member States and this idea can further be extended to India and Pakistan. The perpetual problems like Line of control and Durand Line can be resolve through the concept of a peaceful border. Here I would like to share a maxim of Deng Xiaoping that getting rich is glorious. So can get that glory when there would be peace on the border and borders were used for trade and investment.

## Energy/Tourism/Cultural/Educational Areas of Cooperation

The bulging basket of population and ever decreasing resources have produced a class of populace who are socially extra-conscious about the wellbeing of the people of the subcontinent. The Nobel laureate professors like Dr Abdus Salam and Indian professor Amartya Sen have given special focus to enhance international focus for the social wellbeing of the people. Professor Amartya Sen has emphasized 'welfare economics and social justice for development. All the development models would be successful if the cooperation is enhanced in the fields of energy, tourism, culture and education.

## Role of Russia and China for Regional Integration

Pakistan's historical animosity against India is a clear example of regional unstable relation. Now it has been assumed by some thinkers that the membership of these two hostile States will hamper the efficiency of SCO, or it will further divide the SCO into Chinese and Russian camp (Reeves PhD, 2014). This narrative is a novice but it is a very strong theory presented by some of the political philosophers that SCO may change into a hostile camp between Pakistan and India because Pakistan and India have changed all the regional organizations and International organizations like SAARC, UN, ICJ and most recently OIC's forum into a brawl place between India and Pakistan. So, it will a challenge for Russia and China to pacify the two belligerent States and use the SCO forum not only to resolve the issues but keep it away or from becoming a battleground between these two countries. Shanghai five was that much successful in resolving the regional disputes that it created a 7400 km peaceful border among its member States (Memon, 2006).

China has pragmatically resolved many issues regional issues through peaceful diplomacy and utilizing the regional bilateral and multilateral forums for resolving these issues. SCO has strengthened confidence and good neighbour relations. It has also effectively cooperated in political, socio-economic, educational, cultural are other areas. SCO has also forged new economic and political relations. Regional Anti-Terrorists Structure (RATS) was established at the initiative of Chinese President Jiang Zemin to resolve their issues through active and friendly consultation. According to Article 8 of SCO, the prime focus of this regional organization is on regional peace; countering terrorism, eliminating separatism and overcoming extremism. To meet all these challenges special anti-terrorism set up was established while keeping its Headquarters in Bishkek (Memon, 2006).

**Challenges for the US**

According to Dr Ghulam Ali, the relationship between the US and Pakistan was prompted by a specific strategic goal. Once it was achieved, relations turned lukewarm. In reality, both sides lacked any long term, shared strategic vision, as exists in the case of China-Pakistan (Ali, 2018). Since 2001, SCO has been the known organization for dealing with transnational security threats and pushing for regional coordination of law enforcement and military organizations in Central Asia. Although the USA had announced its "End Game" in Afghanistan due to many issues, it hasn't pulled out its troops from Afghanistan.

The success of SCO is compatible with the US national security goals in the region especially in Central Asia and Afghanistan, but due to its 'zero-sum game' with Russia and China, the US is unwilling to give margin to this regional organization. SCO has the potential to become more successful than European Union. The area and population are the main strength of SCO besides the hydrocarbon resources of the region. The US is feeling that it should stay in the region for a longer time to have a check on the activities of Sino-Russia. This region is the centre of "Heartland" and the US is neither ready to stay here nor willing to loosen its grip on the region.

US has decided to give a leading role to India in the region, in 2011 during its visit to India US Secretary of State Hilary Clinton instigated India to step forward and take the lead role. She explained that the Obama administration wishes to create a friendship between the two countries. Hilary was so ambitious to motivate India to play a leading role in the new century. She also said that the USA is committed to a strong relationship with China and India (Reuters, 2011). These commitments were made at that time when the US was facing the problem of strained relations with Pakistan in the region. India is reluctant to opt between SCO and the US; all the drive of the USA to isolate the big player, India from the SCO is not bearing fruits (Rousseau, 2012).

**Afghanistan's Crucial Role in Regional Integration**

SCO has identified a diverse range of economic cooperation and regional integration is the ultimate aim of this organization. Afghanistan will be the central point of the regional connectivity of South Asia with Central Asia. SCO has a clear policy of non-interference in member's internal issues. A transnational form of trade is a trade between two different countries as a trade partner. In the past trade between different countries was based on the barter system. With all the passing years the importance of Afghanistan has been increasing as the centre of the land corridor between South Asia and the Eurasian region. The fields like science, technology, education, law and order are the main areas of cooperation between the two neighbouring countries.

Two major land routes remain operational throughout the years except for periodical hostilities. Torkham and Chaman entry points are the two-land corridor that can be made part of the future corridor between Pakistan and

Afghanistan most likely through CPEC and SCO. Afghanistan's geographical location is the central connectivity point of the region and it has a common border with Pakistan, China, Tajikistan, Uzbekistan, Turkmenistan and Iran which gives its edge on other regional countries and it proves that without peace in Afghanistan no practicable regional economic integration is possible.

**Indo-Pak areas of Divergence**

Imtiaz Hussian Naz expresses in his book 'Managing spoilers for sustainable peace between India and Pakistan' the theory of spoilers, who spoil the show for different causes. Stedman explains that spoilers themselves are the byproduct of the peace process. The peace process itself generates the opposing viewpoint and they start their anti-peace process initiatives. But the question arises that how these spoilers are made by the peace process. In every game, if there is a winner, then there will be the losers. These losers make compromises on their stance and presume that they have lost it. Due to the fear of their failures, they try to create bottlenecks for the peace process to make it unsuccessful. Spoilers differ from the commitments, which are agreed upon. (Naz, 2019). So, there are many spoilers of relations between India and Pakistan. Due to these spoilers, we had fought four wars and many skirmishes. After the recent event of 27, February 2019 the Pakistan Air Force attacked Indian ground targets inside the LOC. The fear of the nuclear holocaust was that evident that both the nuclear power countries stood in front of each other. It was the first event in history when two nuclear States bombed their adversary openly. During a seminar, I asked a question to Professor Zafar Nawaz Jaspal about the deterrence theory that what is the concept of 'deterrence' after the Indian transgression and Pakistan swift response with bombs? He said that deterrence is still intact because redline of the nuclear threshold was not crossed (Jaspal, 2019).

After the end of WWII, the African and Asian people were liberated from the dominance of imperialism and they embraced freedom due to their struggle (Chander, 2009). After securing freedom from the imperial colonial powers unluckily their countries involved in many territorial disputes and many out of them like Palestine, Areteria, Arakan, Nagorno Karabagh and Kashmir are still unresolved. Many regional and territorial issues need to be resolved by India and Pakistan, besides Kashmir. These issues are Water issue, Siachin, Sir Creek, Border Entry Points, Extremism, drug trafficking etc.

Firgure 16. Siachin Glacier

Source https://www.jagranjosh.com/general-knowledge/what-is-the-siachen-glacier-dispute-1528291952-1

There is a long list of disputes between the two countries. We have fought wars and many skirmishes and we are always at dagger drawn at one another at all the International forums. In the previous seventy years, many golden opportunities are missed to mend the ties and both the nation are not only political rivals but they are unduly fighting in cultural, social, and economic fields.

## Indo-Pak Areas of Cooperation

History is full with the examples of once hostile States changed into friendly nations i.e. Germany and France, Russia and France, Great Britain and Germany, North and South Yemen, Greece and Turkey. All these countries besides many other countries were once arch-rivals of one another but over time, they mend their ties and bury the hatchet. Many outs of these countries are now time-tested friends like Germany and France. Yemen is united into one country. From the very first day, India and Pakistan had hostile posture for one another. Although the majority of the issues starting from the weak governance to border disputes and poverty to low scientific knowledge are common issues of newly liberated countries. Indo-Pak relations are totally off the shadow under the Kashmir issue.

The Kashmir issue has overshadowed all the other issues i.e. Trade, terrorism, poverty, drug trafficking, illiteracy, softening of borders, exchange of scientific knowledge. There is a lot of potential for reviving the trade, cultural and educational relations between India and Pakistan. We had a very good example of China which have a strong "One China" stance about Taiwan but they have mutual trade of US $150 Billion. So, the core issues if they are not resolved then can be capped for the time being to cooperate in other fields.

## Regional Issues

SCO is the best forum to resolve regional issues; especially their efforts are proven successful in the areas like antiterrorism, drug trafficking, soft borders, regional integration, Kashmir, Afghanistan Quagmire and the Indian Ocean. SCO is a successful model where all the disputes are resolved through negotiations and the sovereignty of the country is maintained.

Firgure  17. Map of the BRI Progress

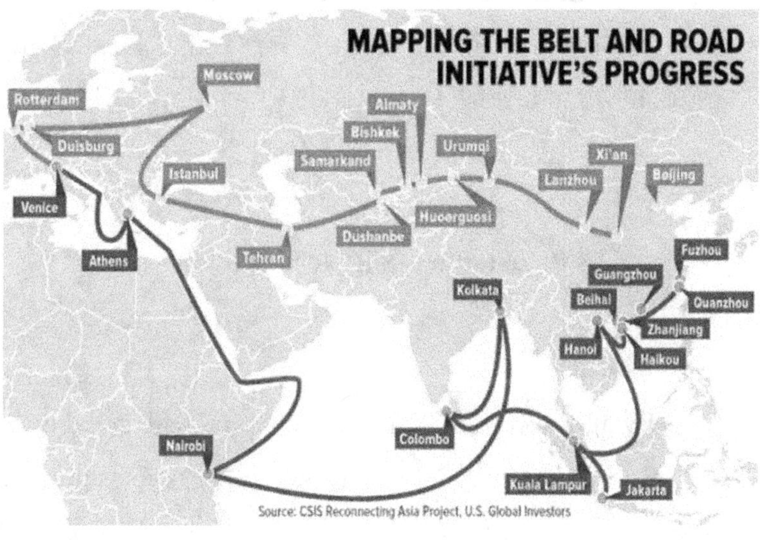


Source.https://www.forbes.com/sites/greatspeculations/2018/09/04/chinas-belt-and-road-initiative

SCO has established a border of peace among its member States. SCO can be utilized as a forum where all these regional issues can be resolve through positive engagement with India.

China's OROB initiative is a map of the future politics of development and Chinese vision has transformed the world. The billions of people are connected for trade and cooperation. There is euphoria in Africa and Latin America. The first Metro train has started its operations in the Ethiopian capital Edessa Baba with Chinese help. Italy is the first G-7 country that had officially signed the BRI project with China which is already an unprecedented move by a western nation and it has shown the confidence of the European nation on Belt and Road (BRI).

## Pakistan's Look North Policy

By all the passing days the economic vulnerability of Pakistan is increasing due to its shrinking economy and smaller capital market. The total GDP of Pakistan is around US$ 300 billion. (Trading Economics, 2019)War against terrorism, insurgency inside Baluchistan, limited energy resources, less investment in human capital, poverty and massive urbanization of big cities has created many economic, social, psychological and political issues for Pakistan. Now Pakistan has to devise a new strategy to change its foreign policy and focus on the countries which are on the north side of Pakistan. China and Russia are given weightage while making or shaping any economic social or strategic strategy.

## Definition

"The look north policy of Pakistan is a foreign policy where China and Russia are given prime importance before devising any policy".

## Importance

In past, Pakistan has made many political blunders and her rudderless foreign policy was a disaster for her. Too much influence inside Afghanistan and joining of the war against terrorism were the decision due to which 70,000 people of this motherland sacrificed their lives for nothing. It badly damaged the economy of Pakistan. Now it is time for Pakistan to rectify its mistakes and set a course of its future foreign policy and strategy. Look North policy is the setting of Pakistan's relations with the North i.e. China, Russia and Central Asia.

## Hidden Incentives

There are a lot of incentives for this policy. The countries present in the North of Pakistan are geographically more integrated with us than any Western country. The countries can provide us with land access to Europe also for trade and education (Russia). China is the progressive economy of the world and the awakening of this dragon has changed the strategic dimensions of world relations. SCO, ECO, CIS, EEU etc. all are based on this region which is in the North of Pakistan. So, Pakistan should declare Look North as the official policy and a strategic road map for her future relations.

## Challenges

SCO has many challenges and these challenges are threats to this new buildup of regional integration are i.e. Regional disputes, Water disputes, Pressure groups, Drugs trafficking, Separatism, Extremism and trust deficit are the main challenges. Partially we can say that SCO is successful in eliminating the maximum of the issues if not all the issues are addressed.

This study has explored the areas of cooperation between Indo-Pak especially as a member of the SCO organization, what types of benefits are associated with it.

What type of regional organization is this and how much success has been achieved by this organization? What are trade and regional cooperation organization? Regional organizations like ASEAN and E.U. have done a lot of success in the fields of regional integration and trade. Their examples are a path of success for other regional organizations. This study has shown that how SCO will change the destiny of this region and how the core conflicts will be resolved through the positive application of neo-functionalism. This study has opened new vistas of knowledge in the field of regional cooperation. The membership of the SCO will be a catalyst of change for the hostile neighbouring States of India and Pakistan. The chronic issues like Kashmir, water disputes, Siachin, Sir Creek, cross border terrorism etc. will be addressed through the positive engagement of Indo-Pak via composite dialogue. Now it would be the responsibility of Russia and China to minimize the tension between both countries.

Special Assistant to the Pakistan Prime Minister on Foreign Affairs Tariq Fatemi once said that our leadership is so much passionate about the friendship with China and they have visited China more than the requirement. They love photo session and off and on trying to grasp the opportunities of those phone sessions, but they are failed to fulfil those commitments. As a result of it, the Chinese are so much disappointed about us, but due to their temperament and nature, they do not project it unnecessarily. The Chinese view against extremism and terrorism is very clear and they categorically announced their stance about it to make us more proactive against them (Small, 2015).

**Discussions and Analysis**

After this extensive research and workout, the scholar has made different analysis and certain judgments are deduced. The trading power China has upgraded into investing power. China is using neo-functionalism to engage other countries through trade and business. After the end of the colonial era, Asia emerged slowly and rose peacefully. The phenomenal rise of India and China as economic power and Russia as a regional power is perceived by the west as a potential threat for the future. In this research, we have studied that the rise of Asia is peaceful and SCO is a model regional organization that is trying to establish new economic order for its regional member countries. China has transformed itself from a 'service economy to a 'knowledge economy. There are diverse fields of cooperation in trade, investment, development, infrastructure, innovation technologies and transportation (SCO, 2019).

SCO will connect India with Central Asia through Pakistan if India joins BRI in future. The USA and all other western powers are airing Indian power out of proportion to make them stand in front of China. The Indian main objective will diminish if they use the policy of confrontation. India is following the policy of 'Connect Central Asia Policy' (Saha, 2014). Pakistan has a long history of friendship with China Pakistan recognized China on 21 May 1951. Many agreements were made between two friendly countries. PIA was the first free world Airline that started operations in mainland China in the 1960s. Pakistan signed the 'Treaty of Friendship, cooperation and Good Neighbor Relations' on 5 April 2005. Free Trade Agreement was signed in July 2007 (Zaki, 2010). CPEC was signed in 2013 and SCO membership was given in 2017. All these agreements boosted already warm relations. Both the countries have developed closer ties in economic, strategic and cultural relations.

According to Ambassador Akram Zaki, the future of Pakistan China relations have three dimensions firstly; the strategic partnership would be converted into comprehensive and long term multidimensional relations, secondly, the private collaboration should be added to State State relations lastly, the bilateral ties should be supported for cooperation at the regional and global level(Zaki, 2010). So, this analysis portrays the picture of future relations and these relations can be developed through CPEC and getting the membership of SCO.

Now it is time to engage India through SCO and its forum. It is too early to say that the SCO forum will be the panacea of all the Indo-Pak relations but it will be a good starter for both the countries to positively engage themselves in the resolutions of the regional issues and devise policies for solutions of the long-term issues. Before the establishment of SCO, Shanghai five resolved all the border issues till June 2000, and then they all Shanghai five-plus Uzbekistan signed SCO in 2001.

The SCO has already resolved many border issues besides that they have enlisted the common problems i.e. terrorism, illegal immigration, drugs trafficking, smuggling and border crimes as common problems of all the member States. So, SCO is an open-door opportunity that has opened many doors of opportunities. SCO is a forum that will counterbalance the European dominancy and American hegemony. The role of NATO will also be counterbalanced by SCO through its regional cooperation and mechanism of collective security.

## Discourses

The studies presented by Prem Shankar Jha is a clear manifestation that this is an Asian century and the two Asian giants will be emerging as the leading economies of the world in near future. (Jha, 2010)This scholar has concluded that the peaceful rise of India is not possible without the solutions to the core issues and it is also in the benefit of Pakistan that India should be engaged on common interests' grounds. SCO will be a regional forum but its success lies in the response of India and Pakistan. The common evils can suppress through this regional forum. The capacity of this forum can also be increased gradually.

## Summary

SCO is a regional cooperation organization. What are the problems and prospects as a Member State, especially for India and Pakistan? India is the main adversary and after joining SCO with India what are the challenges laying ahead for Pakistan? The SCO is representing half of humanity and the leading economies of the world i.e. India and China like emerging and leading economies are the member of this organization.SCO is called the 'Alliance of East'. It is the largest regional organization in the world in term of geographical coverage and population. It is representing the three-fifth of the Eurasian continent (Global Times, 2018).According to Goldman Sachs' report 'Dreaming with BRIC: the path to 2050' Chinese economy will exceed the USA as the world No 1 economy, well before 2050 around 2039. According to this report, China will surpass the USA and India will be the third economic power of the world in the year 2050(Jha, 2010). Pakistan economy will also change from middle-order economies to be among the progressive economies, if and only if the projects of CPEC and SCO are completed well in time. The forum of SCO will not be utilized to brawl with India.

According to National Intelligence Council's 2020 project assessment, China will overtake Russia as the second-largest defence spender after the USA and this will not only increase the sphere of influence of China but will make it the 1st class military superpower. (Jha, 2010)

SCO will be a forum, where nuclear countries like China, India, Russia and Pakistan will be managing their regional affairs and devising a collective policy for international issues. SCO will be a forum where these members' countries will be managing their issues before the provocation of threat. Now after the membership of SCO, it is the responsibility of India and Pakistan to address all the regional issues through bilateral engagement or SCO forum.

If the SCO multilateral forum is actively utilized, the maximum no of regional issues will be resolved. Now the responsibility lies on India and Pakistan to show some maturity. As a big country, more responsibility lies on India to address the real grievances of Pakistan and don't try to intimidate Pakistan. A similar amount of responsibility lies on Pakistan equally to give peace a chance and give time to SCO for the betterment of the population of both countries.

# Chapter Five

# Conclusion

## Findings and Recommendation

### Overview

After research by this scholar, the following findings and conclusions are made which shows that there are spoilers who are creating problems and not letting the normalization process start between India and Pakistan (Naz, 2019). These spoilers are of different categories and types and they have different agendas to spoil the peace process. There are ample opportunities for cooperation between two hostile States, now it is in the benefit of the States and their people that now they are to set aside the concept of permanent foe and they have to take a new start in the right of regional cooperation.

### Findings

The following findings are made after the research and analysis of data;

> SCO is the revival and modification form of the Shanghai five organizations. The two heavyweights Russia and China are the founding members of this

organization and Pakistan and India had joined the member of this organization after a lot of debates.

➤ The importance of SCO has increased many folds after the announcement of Belt and Road (BRI).BRI project has increased the importance of trade in the world.BRI will initially connect 65 countries or almost 4 billion people of the world. After becoming members of the SCO, Pakistan and India can resolve their major problems by this forum.

➤ The SCO has a clear policy of non-interference in the internal affairs of the member States. The UN charter Chapter VIII gives a mandate to the regional organizations. League of Nations was a failed organization but it was the predecessor of the UN. Articles 51 to 54 of the UN charter deals with the rules for regional organizations. India after its independence went closer to China and Nehru was the main architect of that friendship.

➤ The initial friendship between India and China was based on the concept of five rules (Punj Sheel). The friendship euphoria was evaporated when India and China fought a limited war in 1962.

➤ Although Russia is not a superpower it enjoys its 'sphere of influence' in Central Asia. China is the main trade partner of Central Asia and she is exploiting the hydrocarbon and mineral resources of this region. To counter the Russo-Chinese influence USA has made an investment of US $ 2 billion in Afghanistan for the construction of 1800 km roads.

➢ China is increasing its presence in Asia and Africa. SCO will play a decisive role in future relations among its member States. Pakistan and India have the experience of working in SAARC.

➢ The failure of SAARC is a big question mark on its performance and prevailing mistrust between India and Pakistan. According to a scholar Dr Reeves, 'the animosity between Indo-Pak can polarize SCO into Russian and Chinese camps.

➢ The main offshoot of the BRI project in CPEC, which is bringing billions of dollar of investment to Pakistan. According to the WTO, world trade has increased 40 times from 1950 to 2017.WTO has decreased tariffs up to an average of 20 % since the 1960s.

➢ The US is propagating that China is trapping the world into a 'Debt trap'.

➢ SCO is a security and economic cooperation organization.

➢ Western countries consider SCO as a counterweight of NATO eastwards expansion.

- SCO will increase regional prosperity through its long-term projects.
- After securing SCO membership now it is the responsibility of Pakistan to secure maximum projects from China.
- Since 2002 SCO has started military drills.
- SCO has initiated Regional Anti-Terrorism Structure (RATS) in 2002 in Bishkek to counter-terrorism and separatism.
- Besides RATS there is collaboration in many other fields under different ministries i.e. law enforcement, Defense Ministers, interior Ministers.
- Although Russian is sceptical about the Chinese investment in the region China is accommodating their reservations.
- SCO is considered as 'Alliance of Asia' due to its centrality to the Asian continent.
- SCO is the largest regional organization due to its geographical coverage.
- SCO was given observer status in the UN in 2004.
- SCO has further emphasized its cooperation with other regional organizations i.e. ASEAN, Common Wealth of Independence States (CIS) and Collective Security Treaty Organization (CSTO).

- Afghanistan perpetual unrest will hinder stability in the region and it will further deteriorate the region because without peace in Afghanistan there are very bleak chances of success of SCO.
- SCO has established a permanent body for counter-terrorism with Head Quarter at Tashkent.
- Some Western political scholars ridicule the role of SCO in the region by considering it as a mere showpiece where its member heads of the States gather only for a photo session. According to their observation up till now no solid development has been made by the SCO as an international organization.
- SCO has to strongly support the Afghanistan government to strengthen its base and establish friendly relations with Pakistan and India to open its trade links with them.
- SCO can become a panacea against all the ills like Kashmir, Siachin, water disputes etc.
- SCO is playing a stability factor role for Indo-Pak.
- SCO has strongly discouraged its forum to be utilized for quarrels.
- Pakistan enjoys the shortest land access to Central Asia and she links them with the warm waters of the Arabian Sea

- After becoming a member of SCO Pakistan will strengthen the North-South trade and energy corridor passing through Gwadar.

- The TAPI and CASA projects will add up the electricity and hydrocarbon resources of the region. These projects will open a new milestone in the history of Asian cooperation.

- SCO is a forum that will be used for the economic integration of its member States for that purpose another organization naming Eurasian Economic Union (EEU) has already been established in 2014.

- The economic integration projects like Belt and Road initiative (BRI) and China Pakistan Economic Corridor (CPEC) will be the fate changer for India and Pakistan.

- There is a lot of cynical views about the performance of the regional organizations. The unsuccessful international organizations like ECO, OIC and SAARC have many stories to share but the successful organizations like ASEAN, NAFTA and E.U have outshined the stigmatized regional organizations through their performance

- After the expanding role of the World Bank (WB) and International Monitory Fund (IMF) and the debate of the legitimacy of the regional and International organizations has gathered momentum.

➤ From the very first day of its inception Pakistan was in search of true friends (although, in international relations, there is no permanent friend), Pakistan tried to establish its links with the west by joining SEATO and CENTO.

➤ Pakistan blindly cooperated with the USA for making its western allies happy.

➤ Pakistan can connect the world with CARs through its deep seaports and we are the natural land corridor between the Arabian Sea, SCO countries and the Middle East. Pakistan will play a central role to link the North-South energy corridor and trade routes through Gwadar port after the completion of CPEC.

➤ When India will be a stakeholder in this project then it will enhance the stature of Pakistan in the region because Pakistan will be controlling the transit route of these energy projects which will increase the economic vulnerability of India alongside its dependency on Pakistan.

➤ The rehabilitation process in Afghanistan can be initiated through SCO. Health, education and social sector can be improved through SCO.

➤ Pakistan can also strengthen its security apparatus through SCO.

➤ Russia is enjoying its historical and cultural dominancy in the region but China is technically replacing it due to its massive economic growth and China has opened an energy corridor with Central Asia.

➤ China tries to create a safe zone around her territory through international regional organizations both in terms of security and economy. Oil and Gas are abundantly available in Central Asia.

➤ In 1994 at the time of its inception, NAFTA was the biggest free trade market of three countries and it measured $6 trillion and directly affected more than 365 million people.

➤ The trade between India and Pakistan is already underutilized and it can be increased up to US$ 37 billion.

➤ The major fields of cooperation between Indo-Pak can be energy, telecommunications, information, environmental protection and the optimum utilization of natural resources.

➤ These unholy alliances and search for friends had thrown us into the war of Afghanistan.

- Pakistan's strategic location, its military power, its nuclear arsenal and its geopolitical position relative to both India and the rest of the Muslim world

- On 09 June 2017 in Astana during the SCO session, India and Pakistan were given full membership status.

- The emerging economies of China, Russia and India could counterbalance the economies of the United States and its western allies. The use of the Yuan as an international currency among these countries will further counter the power of the Dollar as an international currency and it will weaken the American hegemony and dominancy.

- Kyrgyzstan and Uzbekistan agreed to provide military facilities for the US-led coalition's operations in Afghanistan after they declared war against terrorism in 2001.

- The Central Asian States are pursuing independent foreign policies and their known examples are Turkmenistan, Uzbekistan etc. who have strong control over their domestic policies and have an independent foreign policy.

- Pakistan and India like Russia and the USA are to start an arms limitation dialogue so that they can set budgets for poverty alleviation and social development.

- China has successfully uplifted 850 million people from poverty into the middle class.

- According to World Bank and IMF, there was 21.9 % poverty in India and 29.9 % in Pakistan. The per capita income in Pakistan was US$ 1510 and in India, it was US$ 1584.

- The scrapping of special status and the Balakot incident has intensified relations between the two nuclear states of India and Pakistan.

- The narrow nationalism should be set aside and internationalism should be promoted and the theory of functionalism should be kept in mind for greater cooperation among the regional countries.

- All the development models would be successful for India and Pakistan if the cooperation is enhanced in the fields of energy, tourism, culture and education.

- Shanghai five successful in resolving the regional disputes that it created a 7400 km border which was free from disputes and military buildup.

- Regional Anti-Terrorist Structure (RATS) was established at the initiative of the Chinese President Jiang Zemin to resolve their problems through friendly consultation.

- Afghanistan's geographical location is the central connectivity point of the region and it has a common border with Pakistan, China, Tajikistan, Uzbekistan, Turkmenistan and Iran which gives her edge over other regional countries and it proves that without peace in Afghanistan no practicable regional economic integration is possible.

➢ There are many spoilers of relations between India and Pakistan. Due to these spoilers, we had fought four wars and many skirmishes.

➢ SCO is the best forum to resolve regional issues; especially their efforts are proven successful in the areas like antiterrorism, drug trafficking, soft borders, regional integration, Kashmir, Afghanistan Quagmire and the Indian Ocean.

**Conclusion**

After all the detailed study and data analysis of this research, the following conclusions are made that International Relations are very fragile and short-sighted. Friends can be easily changed with the interests, and the friendship of a State is based on those interests. The friends are not considered permanent neither are foes. Russia and Pakistan were rivals during the cold war. USSR was the leading communist bloc and Pakistan was in the western camp. The notorious event of U-2 happened and Pakistan was marked as an enemy by the USSR. Then Pakistan trapped

USSR in 'Afghanistan Jihad' and Russian was forced out from Afghanistan after the 'Geneva agreement'. Later on, USSR was broken into 15 independent States. The old rivals of 'cold war' and 'Afghan Jihad' are now very good friends and in 2017 the special forces of both the countries jointly exercised in Cherat (KPK, Pakistan) under the title of Druzhba (peace) and the last exercise was done in Krasnodar (Russia).

The lesson from the history of the German and France rivalry is another example of when the arch-rivals of Europe who fought many wars in history become the best friends in Europe and become the pillars of the European Union. How they buried their hatchet and opened new horizons for cooperation? How they had transformed Europe into an island of peace and prosperity? Globalization has shaken the old concepts and distances are evaporated due to transformation into communication. The old communist economies have opened their doors for free-market economies and the authoritarian regimes are dwindling in the Middle East and Africa. China has made miracles by opening a new era of development. The average per capita income of Chinese citizens has increased many folds. The Chinese economy has made miraculous achievements by surpassing the world economies and taking as the second biggest economy of the world. The Belt and Road Initiative (BRI) is the biggest development projects in the world in centuries which will create a turnover of US$ 21 trillion and more than half the population of the world will be joining it. Italy has become the first world economy that has also joined this project. So, development should be the main objective of the governments of the States.

India is an emerging economy of Asia and she is also a member of BRICS countries. The relations between India and Pakistan are based on the "Zero-sum Game". The recent episodes of February 2019 have increased the importance of peace in the region. The two nuclear States are dagger drawn and their sword rattling will be a perpetual bluff for peace in the region. If the issue of Kashmir is not addressed amicably, the peace of this region would be at stake. This recent incident has also shown that how fragile are the peace efforts in this region. Pakistan and India can be engaged through cooperation in all the fields and this process will start when we will optimally utilize the SCO forum besides other regional engagements.

After the elections of Pakistan (2018) and India (2019), the ultra-nationalist and right-wing governments have formed. The PTI government is narrow nationalist according to its agenda and the BJP government is ultra-nationalist in nature. Pakistan is the biggest shareholder in the BRI's offshoot project of CPEC. After securing membership of SCO now Pakistan has to attract more investment from China and other countries in the form of FDI. Peace is very necessary for it and India and Pakistan to have to be set aside the old rivalry and open new doors for cooperation. Then Pakistan can attract more investment from Iran and the Middle East. CPEC can easily be extended to Middle East Iran and Afghanistan. If India would be ready and prepared, she can also be made as part of this investment, which can open a direct land route for India to Central Asia, Afghanistan and onwards to Europe.

SCO has two heavyweights of this region as its founding member. China and Russia have a great influence on this region. After securing the membership of this regional organization now it is the responsibility of India and Pakistan to use this forum to peacefully settle their dispute through a composite dialogue. After securing the membership and signing the different agreements India will also become the stakeholder in these projects then it will enhance the stature of Pakistan because Pakistan will be controlling the transit routes of the energy projects which can also increase the economic vulnerability of India alongside its dependency on Pakistan. TAPI and CASA will replenish the dwindling energy resources of Pakistan.

The oil and gas-rich states of Central Asia will fulfil the energy needs of South Asia.SCO is the proper body that will facilitate these interactions and will provide the forum where the major fields of cooperation between India and Pakistan will be discussed.

The major fields of cooperation between Indo-Pak can be energy, telecommunication, information, environment protection and the utilization of natural resources. Besides that, the poverty elevation, cultural exchange, scientific knowledge, counters terrorism, extremism and separatism would be the areas of immediate concern for both the neighbouring countries. Economic integration is the most useful manifestation of the present age. SCO is the forum that would be utilized for the economic integration for its member States. The successful economic unions like European Economic Community (EEC), NAFTA, and ASEAN are a few examples of successful models. In 2014 Eurasian Economic Union (EEU) was established for the economic integration of the regional countries. The other regional organizations like the Commonwealth of Independence States (CIS) and Collective Security Treaty Organization (CSTO) have also extended their hands for cooperation with SCO.

Regional Anti-Terrorism Structure (RATS) is a forum for counter-terrorism and separatism. This centre provides intelligence to the member States regarding terrorism and counter-terrorism strategies are devised and periodic exercises and arms drills are also done. Although the SCO mandate makes restricted to non-interference in the internal matters of the member States China and Russia can exercise their influence on India and Pakistan to start a comprehensive composite dialogue to resolve their core disputes.

Afghanistan quagmire is the souring wound of Asia and it is the unsolved problem of the region. If there is no peace in Afghanistan then there are very bleak chances of success of other regional initiatives. SCO should focus on this issue because the strategic location of Afghanistan is very important and all the major land connectivity projects i.e. CASA and TAPI would be passing from it. Afghan Transit Trade (ATT) can be made as to the part of CPEC and the network of Pakistan motorways can be extended to Kabul. Railways and highways can link it from Qandahar and Jalalabad.

Yuan is the Chinese currency but after the enhanced role of SCO, this would replace the dollar in the region for international exchange. Yuan has already been playing this role in the CPEC projects where it is used as an alternative to the dollar. The Yuan as an international currency in the SCO common market would not only curtail the influence of the dollar in the Asian market but will also save the foreign exchange of the smaller countries.

## Recommendations

After concluding through research on the topic "Shanghai Cooperation Organization: Problems and Prospects for Indo-Pak Relations" the following recommendations are drawn from research that The world relations are now transforming from mere strategic to economic incentive-based and China has this honour that they has started the game of positive competition in the world and it has tactfully utilized the concept of 'functionalism' where it has engaged all its friends and foes into trade and business. Their biggest rival like the USA and their disputed land like Taiwan and fully engaged with them in the field of business. SCO is a regional forum which was initiated by Russia and China and these two heavyweights are the founding member of this organization.

Pakistan and India are the two regional rival players who have a long history of wars and antagonism. Due to their chequered relations, they were made a member of SCO after a lot of deliberations by other member States. The importance of the region has increased after the announcement of the Belt and Road Initiative (BRI). Now Pakistan is the biggest shareholder of this project due to the China Pakistan Economic Corridor (CPEC) billions of dollars are invested in Pakistan. After securing membership of SCO now Pakistan can utilize this forum to build her international positive picture and attract more investment not only from China but also from other international investors.SCO is an organization where India is also a member of this organization and now it is the responsibility of Pakistan and India to utilize this forum for trust-building. The presence of regional players can make space for them and the role of Russia and China will conveniently arrange composite dialogue where all the chronic issue i.e. Kashmir, Siachin, terrorism, water disputes, smuggling, cross border terrorism would be discussed.

The SCO has opened doors for regional cooperation among its member countries. The Central Asian States are the hydro-carbon rich States and through SCO agreements they access to these countries can be utilized for trade and oil and gas explorations. The Russian influence is still present in the region and the Chinese are also increasing their influence in the region so it is time to open land and air routes with the Central Asian States. All the Central Asian States are landlocked and they are in desperate need of a warm port that would be navigation able round the year. Gwadar Port and Port Qasim can play this role even Gwadar port it is providing the shortest land access to the warm waters. In the future Indian and Iranian ports i.e. Chahbhar, Bombay and Port Abbas can also be added for trade. When India will be a stakeholder in this project then it will enhance the stature of Pakistan in the region because Pakistan will be controlling the transit route of these energy projects which will increase the economic vulnerability of India alongside its dependency on Pakistan. Pakistan can play a vital role in the connectivity of the North-South trade route which would be passing through Gawadar. China is the main trade partner of Central Asian countries and it is exploiting the hydro-carbon of this region. The oil and gas-rich countries like Kazakhstan and Turkmenistan can fulfil the energy needs of India and Pakistan although TAPI and CASA agreements were signed long ago they are still not materialized. Now, this is the time when we are to revive these projects and SCO is the forum where we can negotiate for the revival and start of these projects. The major fields of cooperation between Indo-Pak can be energy, telecommunications, information, environmental protection and the optimum utilization of natural resources.

The membership of the regional organizations like SAARC and ECO had brought nothing for us and they partially remained unsuccessful organizations. SCO is a forum that will be used for the economic integration of its member States for that purpose another organization naming Eurasian Economic Union (EEU) has already been established in 2014. Now SCO is a forum where many evils of the region like extremism, terrorism and separatism would be addressed with many other issues. The other regional organizations like ASEAN, Common Wealth of Independence States (CIS) and Collective Security Treaty Organization (CSTO) have also extended their hands towards SCO for cooperation. So, SCO would be playing a more important role in future.

SCO has initiated Regional Anti-Terrorism Structure (RATS) in 2002 in Bishkek to counter-terrorism and separatism. This centre provides intelligence to the member States regarding terrorism and counter-terrorism strategies are devised and periodic exercises and arms drills are also done. Some Western political scholars ridicule the role of SCO in the region by considering it as a mere showpiece where its member heads of the States gather only for the photo session. According to their observation up till now no solid development has been made by the SCO as an international organization. This myth can be broken by SCO through its initiative for peace in the region and Kashmir. Although the SCO mandate makes restricted to non-interference in the internal matters of the member States China and Russia can exercise their influence on India and Pakistan to start a comprehensive composite dialogue to resolve their core disputes.

The rehabilitation process in Afghanistan can be initiated through SCO. Health, education and social sector can be improved through SCO. Pakistan can extend its role for the promotion of peace in Afghanistan through SCO and Afghan Transit Trade (ATT) can be made as to the part of CPEC. In the CPEC project, Yuan is set as an international currency and all the exchange is made through it. This model of Yuan as an exchange currency can be extended to all SCO member States. The emerging economies of China, Russia and India could counterbalance the economies of the United States and its western allies. The use of the Yuan as an international currency among these countries will further counter the power of the Dollar as an international currency and it will weaken the American hegemony and dominancy in the region. Through it the emerging economies of China, Russia Pakistan and India could counterbalance the economies of the United States and its western allies. The use of the Yuan as an international currency among these countries will further counter the power of the Dollar as an international currency and it will weaken the American hegemony and dominancy.

With the initiative of Pakistan and under the support of Russia and China, Pakistan and India should start an arms limitation dialogue like Russia and the USA, so that they can set budgets for poverty alleviation and social development. The arms control dialogue is necessary to bridge the trust gap between the two nuclear rival countries. The dialogue will end or will make limited the mutually assured destruction (MAD). Narrow nationalism should be set aside and internationalism should be promoted and the theory of functionalism should be kept in mind for greater cooperation between India and Pakistan.

SCO will be a ray of hope if all the development models would be successful for India and Pakistan if the cooperation is enhanced in the fields of energy, tourism, culture and education. Shanghai five successful in resolving the regional disputes that it created a 7400 km peaceful border among its member States and stakes holders.SCO is the best forum to resolve regional issues, especially their efforts are proven successful in the areas like antiterrorism, drug trafficking, soft borders, regional integration, Kashmir, Afghanistan Quagmire and the Indian Ocean.

# Chapter Six

# Work Cited

## Overview

All the credible sources and known source of knowledge were used to explore the areas of research. During this research, a scholar has consulted different books, articles, interviews, seminars and face to face question-answer sessions. Scholar has identified the existing gap between already research works of the scholars. The scholar has researched under the title of, "Shanghai Cooperation Organization (SCO) membership problems and prospects for India and Pakistan". The books and articles of different scholars from India, Pakistan, China, Russia and western countries were consulted along with different press release, periodicals and interviews. Their historical antagonism was these two rivals will remain the same in the future, rather few were of this opinion that SCO will also become the prey of this hatred and either it will remain aloof itself from the issues of India and Pakistan or it will split into two hostile camps, one being supported by Russia and second being supported by China.

While organizing this research the writer has explored those opportunities which are still not availed by these two countries. The SCO forum has been an open opportunity for them. In this study, different data graphs and maps are used to show the opportunities lying ahead for us. The Indian aggressive posture and repeated denial of dialogue with Pakistan is the key issue to denial and the leading factor which worsen the effects of the 'zero-sum game'. This study will show how this game between two rivals can be changed into a 'non-zero-sum game' and then into a 'win-win game'.

**Ghulam Ali PhD** (2nd Edition 2018)Dr Ali in his book 'China Pakistan Relations' discuss the relations of Pakistan with China, he is an area expert of China and fellow of the Department of South Asia Studies, Peking University. His book examines relations between Pakistan and China. He takes a historical approach and finds the international and regional factors which cause greater economic cooperation. He has deeply studied SCO and CPEC and discussed their effects on the friendship of both countries. Overall the point of view of Dr Ghulam Ali is very pragmatic about the success of Pakistan China relations. He has shed light on the chronological order of the relations between two friendly friends whose friendship is also time-tested and has gone through all types of ups and downs.

**Jeffery Reeves PhD** (2014) In his article has emphasized the concept that SCO will act as a security provider organization for the region. The USA was going to start 'End Game' in2014 but still, they are present in the region and they wanted to have a strong presence in the region so that they can have an eye on the region. Dr Reeves believes that if the USA will leave the area there would be chaos in the region. That's why the presence of the USA will suppress all types of terrorism from the region and then regional integration would be helpful. The viewpoint of Dr Reeve is a bit partial because he is still of this opinion that the USA should have a strong presence in the region. Although it is very detrimental to the peace of the region the presence of the USA is the leading cause of chaos in the region. The vacuum that would be created after the American pullout would be filled by the strong effort of the regional countries like Pakistan, China, Iran and Russia.

**M. Akram Zaki** (2010). The book is written by this senior diplomat on China who has spent many years of his life as a specialist of China, as a diplomat he observed the rise of China from a middle-class country to a first-class economic superpower and power hub of the world economy. His research deals with the status of China today and tomorrow, from independence to fourth-generation leadership, economic development, Chinese relations with different countries and Pak-China cooperation in the 21st century. This book is a very small booklet with having a total of 113 pages. The analysis presented by Akram Zaki very simple and based on his observations while staying in China. He presented his analysis of the emerging future picture in chapter 'future scenario' where he presented the next level of relations of both countries but again this known scholar also missed the dimension that if India also joins some regional bloc like SCO what would be its outcome. So, the researcher will cover this area in his present research.

**Rizwan Zeb** (2006) writes in his article that SCO is a very important organization. CARs will also play a vital role against terrorism. Pakistan has established cordial relations with CARs and it will be important for the maximizing of gains. Peace in the region is possible when there would be peace in landlocked Afghanistan. All the Central Asian Republics States are the main source of hydrocarbon, fossil fuel and ample trade opportunities for Pakistan and India are there. He predicted that in near future Pakistan will become a member of SCO, but he sadly accepted that the trade of Pakistan with SCO countries is below their potential. So now in our research, we have explored the new areas of economic integration and problem solving for member countries under SCO.

**Ivan Campbell** (2013) in this article writer discusses that historically India is enjoying special historical relations, especially with USSR. Now India is going to diversify its energy requirements and has sustained economic growth. Central Asia is the power hub of the world due to its ample availability of 'fossil fuel'. In 2012 India had launched the 'Connect Central Asia Policy' that's why stronger political relations were established with all the CARs, Afghanistan and Iran. There were two major objectives of India to connect with Central Asia: - Firstly, securing and diversifying Indian economic growth needs by injecting energy from Central Asia and Secondly, to have a check on the expansion of radical Islam. The focus of Ivan Cambell is very narrow. According to Robert D Kaplan, India's history is "the story of invasion from north-westerly direction". So, he has seen the Indian relations with the region in the security paradigm. Our focus of research is to explore the areas where both the regional players can maximize their gains and minimize their losses.

**Zhao Xiaodong** (2012) in his article has focused on the counter-terrorism efforts made by SCO. He has discussed the mechanism of RATS where all the member States discuss their efforts to eliminate extremism and terrorism. According to Zhao, SCO has covered a large area and its challenges are multidimensional. To meet the challenges regular interaction of the States officials are made and counter-terrorism exercises are made periodically. This article is the best available information regarding the counter-terrorism efforts made by the SCO. After becoming a member of this counter-terrorism setup, Pakistan and India will jointly resolve their counter-insurgency and counter-terrorism efforts.

**Jafar Riaz Kataria and Anum Naveed** (2014) in their article discussed the social and economic linkages between regional countries. The friendship of these neighbours is the most successful model organization in the world which is dealing with all the major areas like, trade, military exercises, intelligence sharing etc. China has the biggest army in the world and they are the biggest importer and exporter of the world. There are five major policy principles of Chinese foreign policy for South Asia which is based on the five principles for peaceful coexistence.

**Palmer & Perkins** (2010) In this book both the distinguished writers have dedicated a complete chapter on "The New Regionalism" where they have discussed the pros and cons of regionalism and different successful regional models. Regionalism was also present before WWI but it expanded after WWII. Here they have discussed the

Organization of the American States, EFTA, GATT, NATO, SEATO, Colombo Plan and ASEAN.

**Jeffrey Newnham and Graham Evans** (1998) this unique reference book 'The Penguin dictionary of International Relations' about International Relations and besides all the core theories and concepts and trade organizations are briefly discussed in it. According to Professor J.E. Spence, it is "cogently argued and lucidly expressed. The scholarship is impeccable". So, it is the best and versatile handbook available to study. So, it provides handy knowledge about International Relations, its theories and events from history.

**Moonis Ahmar** (2003) has discussed the regional integration of SAARC countries under the regional organization of SAARC. He has discussed the importance of territorial organizations for the prevention of terrorism. According to his point of view, the member States of SAARC have realized the threat of terrorism and its effects on the territorial integrity of States. Now after the membership of SCO, these threats can be curbed by utilizing the Chinese and Russian model of regional cooperation.

**Francis Fukuyama** (2015) is one the most distinguished scholar of the present age and his most famous work was his concept of 'End of History' which had opened new doors for discussions about the victory of western liberalism and the free market economy as the ultimate future of the world. But his concept was strongly rejected by the anti-thesis title "Clash of civilizations". Still, his work is the most important political work on political thought in at least a generation. His book covers all the continents and also discusses the governance history of China. Francis Fukuyama presented China as an authoritarian state controlling all the affairs of its citizens and subjugating their freedom of will and having checks on social media and freedom of expression.

**Jafar Riaz Kataria** (2014) Kataria has discussed in his article that East Asian economies are the world best and successful models of regional trade. He has discussed the Sino-Pak relations while dividing them into different eras. He has discussed the events in chronological order to understand the events and happenings. He has also discussed the trade relations of China with Pakistan.

**Nicola P. Contessi** (2016) Contessa has shed light in his article on the trans-regional links of Central Asia. According to his research, the Belt and Road Initiative (BRI) will generate a total of US $ 21.1 trillion of economic turnover. He further pointed out that this involvement of

Asia will grow into Pan-Asia multilateralism. It will further integrate Asia with Eurasia.

**Stephen Aris (2008)** In his article discusses that SCO has played a very major role in the thaw of the relations between China and Russia. He believes that Russian and Chinese have many common interests in the region so there is no chance of tension between these two powers. The relevancy of this organization would enhance when the other members will consider it as their problem solver mechanism.

**Nadine Godehardt** (2016) has presented this idea that after Francis Fukuyama 'End of History' concept, China is the alternate model and emerging as the economic power hub of the world. President Xi has strongly supported his vision of opening the world for trade. Half of the world populations would be integrated through this connectivity.

**James Macbride** (2015) Han dynasty in China was the first rulers who opened 'Silk Road' for world trade. Now new Silk Road has been initiated by the present Chinese government. Turkmenistan has the second largest deposits of gas in the world. TAPI and other regional energy and trade projects are in pipelines. China is going to adopt more assertive behaviour.

**Prem Shankar Jha** (2010) in his book, Prem Shankar Jha has focused his research on Indo-China economic rise as a world power States. He has made a certain comparison about the economic condition of India and China, especially he has analyzed the rise of these political and trade rivals after they disbanded their authoritarian economics to market-based economies after the year 2000 relevant data has been discussed.

**Andrew Small** (2015) in his book discusses that China Pakistan plays a very pivotal position in Asia. Pakistan plays a central point in the foreign policy of China and the geopolitics of Asia is uncompleted without the presence of these two players. The role of these two countries has been increased very much after inking BRI and CPEC. India has been made vulnerable after this strategic shift of Pakistan into the economic future map of the world being led by China. Now India has very limited options either it has to extend its hands for cooperation towards Pakistan and China or join the bandwagon of America. The chances of success are limited in it. Only the way towards success is passing from the economic integration of Asia. Time is slipping from the hands of India.

**Minhas Majeed, Ahmed Rashid, Saira Ijaz and Umeer Farwa** (2016) in their compiled book they analyze that CPEC is lifeline for the energy striven country Pakistan. The success of this project lies in the commitments of the succeeding governments of Pakistan to fulfil their commitments made with China. This book has also illustrated maps of the different CPEC projects; the renowned scholars' work has been compiled in this book. S M Hali, Muhammad Khan, Li Xiguang and five other scholars have shared their point of view regarding CPEC and its success. CPEC is the future of Pakistan; if only this project is completed it will make Pakistan a regional economic power.

**Overview**

The theoretical framework of this research has been based on Neo-functionalism and Realism. These two theories clearly define the objectives of the States and the utilization of the relations for greater benefits of the State. The survival and re-emergence of Russia and the pragmatic utilization of the Neo-functionalism approach of China in the form of SCO and Belt and Road Initiative (BRI) are outstanding. China is maintaining One China policy but has a trade of US$ 150 Billion with Taiwan in 2018 which accounts for 30 of total Taiwan's total trade with China (Albert, 2019). Pakistan and India can follow this example and they can open new vistas of cooperation.US is the main player in Central Asia and it has tried to cover the vacuum created after the fall of the USSR but China has contained discreetly its influence. The presence of the USA in Afghanistan is a problem for the emergence of rising Asia. The scholars are agreed on this that the 21st century is the Asia Century.

The hostile States have a long history of minimizing their gains and maximizing their losses Germany and France, France and Great Britain, Russia and Great Britain and USSR and USA are very clear examples of it. Now the strategists are of this opinion that the real gains are economic gains. China wisdom has taken it as a pathway and their leader Deng Xiaoping had this insight in the eighties and he transformed the structure of their closed economy of China into an open economy. Now China is the trade hub of the world and SCO like organizations has quelled the phenomenon that communist economies are stagnant economies. A project like the "Belt and Road initiative" is connecting 50 % of the world population. It is the biggest trade initiative made by any country through its 68 countries and four Billion population of the world would be connected and SCO will act as an umbrella organization and around 120 and organizations has joined it till now (Malik, 2019).SCO is a successful model to quell Regionalism, Extremism, Drug Trafficking and Separatism. The charter of SCO gives opportunity to the member States that they are sovereign in all of their internal matters.

The theory of Neo-functionalism was applied to Indo-Pak relations, that how can we utilize this theory to enhance economic relations between these countries. The interdependency will compel them to cooperate more in all the fields and resolve their issues through dialogue and interaction. Shanghai Cooperation Organization (SCO) is the best example of this which has created a 'Spillover process' where hostile States gradually set aside their rivalries and started depending on one another. Their economic interdependence has refrained them from engaging in any hot wars and all the issues are amicably resolved. The EU, NAFTA and ASEAN are the best examples of this process where regional economic integration has played a role in regional cooperation.

## Summary

The 21st century the century of peaceful cooperation, now the battlegrounds are changed and now these battles are fought on economic fronts. Science and technology along with globalization have shrunken the distances among humans and it led to the concept of a global economy and 'six degrees of separation. Now due to the use of the fastest social media like 'facebook' and 'twitter' have lessened this connection to one to two degrees and every two humans can be connected through this degree of relation(The Guardian, 2008). The revolution in the field of information technology has virtually limited the land boundaries and other impediments. Here in this research, we will discuss that how Pakistan and India can positively utilize the forum of SCO as member States and not only enhance their cooperation in different fields but also resolve their core disputes. The SCO and Belt and Road Initiative (BRI) will change the future of this area. China Pakistan Economic Corridor (CPEC) will not only be the 'Game changer' rather it would be a 'fate changer' for Pakistan. Sun Tzu said in his book 'Art of War' that the greatest art to subdue your enemy is without fighting (Tzu, 2000).

If we compare Realism with Neo-Functionalism then have to make a clear comparison of it. Realism focuses on Military forces and Economic tools, but Neo-Functionalism focuses on economic instruments as the area of cooperation and competition. Neo-functionalism has focused on minor challenges i.e. trade, unemployment, substantial growth, technology transfer. So, this theory has the maximum utilization for this concept and we have applied this for our research.

# Bibliography

Akine, D. S. (2010). The Shanghai Cooperation Organization: Networking Organisation for a Networking Organization. Global Strategy Forum, 6-10.

Albert, E. (2019, October 04). CFR. Retrieved October 20, 2019, from www.cfr.org: https://www.cfr.org/backgrounder/china-taiwan-relations

Ali, D. G. (2018). China-Pakistan relations A Historical Analysis. Karachi: Oxford.

Anna Matveeva, A. G. (September,2008). The SCO, A Regional Organisation in the Making. Crisis States Research Centre LSE.

AP. (2019, May). Aljazeera. Retrieved May 28, 2019, from www.aljazeera.com: https://www.aljazeera.com/news/2019/05/china-increase-overseas-military-bases-pentagon-report-190503065146243.html

APP. (09 June 2017). Dawn.

Aris, S. (Sept 2008). Russian-Chinese relations through the lens of SCO. Russia/NIS Center ifri Paris.

Arpi, C. (2015, August 05). Indian Defence Review. Retrieved May 10, 2019, from www.indiandefencereview.com: http://www.indiandefencereview.com/spotlights/the-panchsheel-agreement/

Basit, A. (2019, April 10). One day National Conference on Strategic Stability in South Asia: Emerging Challenges. (Haroon, Interviewer)

BBC. (2019, May 06). Retrieved May 06, 2019, from www.bbc.com: www.bbc.com

Chander, P. (2009). International Relations. India: Cosmos Bookhive.

CNN. (1997, April 23). Retrieved October 25, 2019, from www.cnn.com: http://edition.cnn.com/WORLD/9704/23/russia.china/

Cohen, A. (2006, September 07). The dragon looks west: China and the SCO. The Heritage Lectures, pp. 1-8.

Commerce. (n.d.). Retrieved October 23, 2019, from www.commerce.gov.pk: http://www.commerce.gov.pk/about-us/trade-agreements/pak-china-free-trade-agreement-in-goods-investment/

Contessi, N. P. (2016). ". Journal of Eurasian Studies, 395-410.

DPPA. (2019). Retrieved May 15, 2019, from www.dppa.un.org: https://dppa.un.org/en/shanghai-cooperation-organization

Elanor, A. (2019, October 04). CFR. Retrieved October 31, 2019, from www.cfr.org: www.cfr.ogr/backgrounder/china-taiwan-relations

Fukuyama, F. (2015). Political Order and Political Decay. In F. Fukuyama, Political Order and Political Decay (p. 378). New York: Farrar, Straus and Giroux.

Global Times. (2018, June 10). Retrieved October 25, 2019, from www.globaltimes.cn: www.globaltimes.cn/content/1106373.shtml

Grainger, S. (2014, April). Challenges and the future direction of the Shanghai Cooperation Organisation., (pp. 9-11). Singapore.

Greg, D. A. (2004). European Union Policy Responses to the Shanghai Cooperation organisation. EIAS Publications BP 02/04.

Haas, M. d., & Putten, F.-P. V. (2007). The Shanghai Cooperation Organisation. Netherlands Institute of International Relations, 41.

Hughes, L. (2014). So, What if India Becomes a Member of the SCO? Strategic Analysis Paper.

Hurworth, E. (2019, June 19). CNN. Retrieved October 30, 2019, from www.cnn.com:
www.google.com/amp/s/amp.cnn/2019/06/19/health/india-china-world-population-intl-hnk/index.html

Inc Encyclopedia. (2019). Retrieved October 23, 2019, from www.inc.com: www.inc.com.encycopedia.nafta.html

Jafaz Riaz Kataria, A. N. (volume 29 No 2 July-Dec 2014). South Asian Studies, 395-410.

Jaspal, Z. N. (2019, April 10). One day National Conference on Strategic Stability in South Asia: Emerging Challenges. (Haroon, Interviewer)

Jha, P. S. (2010). India and China the battle between soft and hard power. New Dehli: Penguin Group India.

Khan, M. M., Malik, A. R., Ijaz, S., & Farwa, U. (2016). China-Pakistan Economic Corridor, A Game Changer. In China-Pakistan Economic Corridor, A Game Changer (p. 164). Islamabad: The Institute of Strategic Studies.

Khan, S. (n.d.). Stabilization of Afghanistan US-NATO strategy and the Role of SCO. Institute of Strategic Studies.

Kucuk, Z. F. (2009, September). Shanghai cooperation organization and its role. The graduate school of natural and applied sciences, p. 60.

Laumulin, M. (2006, July). SCO as a geopolitical bluff; A view from Astana. ifri Rearch programme.

Lindsay, H. (2014). So, What if India Becomes a Member of the SCO?

Livemint. (2016, September 25). Retrieved October 23, 2019, from www.livemint.com.

Malik, D. A. (2019, July 03). Pakistan Today. Retrieved September 06, 2019, from www.pakistantoday.com: https://www.pakistantoday.com.pk/2019/07/03/the-diversified-bri/

Matveeva, A., & Giustozzi, A. (2008, September). The SCO: The regional organization in the making. Crisis States Research Centre, LSE.

Mcbride, J. (2015, 05 26). Building The New Silk Road. www.cfr.org. Retrieved from www.cfr.org.

Memon, D. A. (2006). A S I A P A C I F I C, A RESEARCH JOURNAL OF FAR EAST & SOUTHEAST ASIA AREA STUDY CENTRE, p. 80.

Mishra, A. R. (2018, September 20). Retrieved October 15, 2019, from www.livemint.com.

Nadine, G. (2016). No end of History, Chinese alternate concept of International Order. Retrieved from www.ssoar.info.

Naz, I. H. (2019). Managing spoilers for sustainable peace between India and Pakistan. Karachi: paramount books.

Niazi, T. (2006, May 06). Asia Between China and India. The Asia-Pacific Journal | Japan Focus Volume 4 | Issue 5.

Rabbani, G. (2016). Contemporary International Relations. In G. Rabbani. Jhangir World Times Publications.

Reeves PhD, J. (2014). SCO: A Tenable Provider of Security in Post 2014 Central Asia. Asia Pacific Center for Security Studies.

Rehman, D. M. (2014). Significance of SCO ; Pakistan perspective. Marginal Papers, 65-84.

Rousseau, R. (2012). India, the SCO and Potential Shift in the Asian Axis of Power.

SAARC. (n.d.). Retrieved May 12, 2019, from www.saarc.org: https://www.saarc-sec.org/

Saha, S. (2014, October 17). East Asia Forum. Retrieved October 23, 2019, from www.eastaisforum.org: www.eastasiaforum.org/2014/10/17/the-future-of-the-sco/31/10/19

SCO. (2019, October 23). Retrieved October 25, 2019, from www.eng.sectsco.org: www.eng.sectsco.org/sectsco.org/news/2019/10/23/590726.html

Singh, N. D. (22 March 2016). India's SCO Membership: looking forward to opportunities in the Caspian region. Centre of Air Power Studies.

Small, A. (2015). The China Pakistan Axis. London: Hurts & Company, London.

The Guardian. (2008, August 03). Retrieved September 15, 2019, from www.theguardian.com: https://www.theguardian.com/technology/2008/aug/03/internet.email

Times of India. (2019). Retrieved from www.timeofindia.com.

Trading Economics. (2019). Retrieved May 25, 2019, from www.tradingeconomics.com: https://tradingeconomics.com/pakistan/gdp

Tzu, S. (2000). The Art of War. Allende Online Publishing.

UN. (2019, October 16). Retrieved October 16, 2019, from www.un.org: https://www.un.org/en/sections/un-charter/chapter-viii/index.html

UN legal. (2019). Retrieved October 20, 2019, from www.legal.un.org: http://legal.un.org/repertory/art51.shtml

United Nations. (n.d.). Retrieved September 12, 2019, from www.un.org: https://www.un.org/en/sections/un-charter/chapter-viii/index.html

WB. (2019, April 08). Retrieved July 08, 2019, from www. world bank.org: www.worldbank.org/en/country/china/overview

Williams, M. (2012, March 15). The Guardian. Retrieved June 12, 2019, from www.theguardian.com: https://www.theguardian.com/commentisfree/cifamerica/2012/mar/15/obama-gets-afghan-endgame.

Wikipedia. (n.d.). Shanghai Cooperation Organzation. Retrieved from www.wikipeda.com: www.wikipedia.org/wiki/Shanghai_cooperation_Organization?wprov=sfl a1

World Bank. (2019, October 01). Retrieved October 15, 2019, from www.worldbank.org:
https://www.worldbank.org/en/country/china/overview

WTO. (2019, May 08). Retrieved 2019 08 May 2019, from www.wto.com: www.wto.org

Xiaodong, Z. (2012). The SCO and Counter-Terrorism cooperation. Asia Paper Institute for Security and Development Policy.

Zaki, M. A. (2010). China of today and tomorrow, Dynamics of relations with Pakistan. In A. Zaki, China of today and tomorrow, Dynamics of relations with Pakistan (p. 39). Islamabad: IPS.

Zeb, R. (volume 4, No 4 2006). Pakistan and the Shanghai Cooperation Organisation. China and Eurasian Forum Quarterly, 51-60.